THE DOLOMITES

Also available in the Plant Hunters series:

THE VALLEY OF FLOWERS by F. S. Smythe
Introduction by Geoffrey Smith

PLANT HUNTING ON THE EDGE OF THE WORLD
by F. Kingdon Ward
Introduction by Geoffrey Smith

PRIMULA MINIMA

THE
DOLOMITES

KING LAURIN'S GARDEN

BY REGINALD FARRER
INTRODUCTION BY GEOFFREY SMITH

CADOGAN BOOKS
LONDON

First published in Great Britain in 1913
by Adam and Charles Black

This edition published 1985 by
Cadogan Books Ltd
16 Lower Marsh, London SE1 7RJ

British Library Cataloguing in Publication Data

Farrer, Reginald
    The Dolomites: King Laurin's garden.—(Plant
hunters)
    1. Dolomite Alps (Italy)—Description and
travel—Guide-books
    I. Title
    914.5'38049   DG975.D68

ISBN 0-946313-17-2

Printed and bound in Great Britain by
Biddles Ltd, Guildford and King's Lynn

INTRODUCTION TO THIS EDITION

On the memorial to Reginald Farrer which stands in the garden at Clapham he is described as 'Author, traveller, botanist, and flower painter'. Farrer was, indeed, all of these, yet with a gift of interpreting and recording his experiences in print which makes him, if not unique, then one of a very select band.

Let me confess to a regard for the man which borders on veneration. Reading his books fired a youthful interest in mountain flowers which has lasted over forty years. In Farrer's own words; 'In this book though, I am holding out the hand of my company not only to my gardening friends but all those who love the hills in general, but know nothing special of their flowers.' Such was my case when first reading 'The Dolomites', which I bought for five shillings in a Norwich bookshop. Love of the hills is something I was born with; an interest in flowers grew from a childhood environment—in the writings of Farrer, which reveal that combination of the practical and the romantic, I discovered a stimulus to my own enthusiasm for Alpine plants. His descriptions of flowers and scenery are sharp, graphic and percipient to a degree that, at times, achieves a spiritual enjoyment beyond the normal senses. His books are also a fine antidote to pedestrian, strictly functional, gardening tomes.

Some years ago, on the 50th anniversary of Farrer's death, I was asked to give a talk on the man, and to attempt an evaluation of his contribution to gardening. Weeks spent studying his letters, field notes, diaries, and other memorabilia—often sitting engrossed into the early hours of the morning—far from reducing my high opinion of Farrer as an author served only to reinforce it; for his letters home read like adventure stories.

Who was Farrer? and what set of circumstances formed the man's character? The first question is easy enough to answer. Farrer was born in 1880 of a modestly wealthy, land owning family living at the time in Clapham, a village lying snugly sheltered below Ingleborough in Yorkshire. A hare lip, unfortunate disability though it undoubtedly must have been for a young boy to suffer, may have proved the one single factor which influenced the whole of his adult life—though this can, of course, only be conjecture. Owing to the malformed lip he was educated at home until going up to Oxford. The interest in botany, already apparent at the age of eight, combined with the opportunity to put into practice the skills acquired in the classroom must have played an important part in laying a foundation as solid-rooted as Ingleborough itself on which to build the experience of later years.

Given the task of choosing a suitable environment in which to nurture an embryo botanist, Clapham would be high on any list I would suggest. The basic rock from which the soil has been formed is predominantly limestone, yet a survey has shown several different soil types, including acid loam, suitable for lime hating plants. The thriving population of Rhododendrons established in the woodland bordering Clap Beck were grown from seed sent home by Farrer from China. The area offers a cross section of growing conditions, a fact reflected in the richness and diversity of the native flowers. Several plants listed in the catalogue issued by Farrer from the Craven Nurseries were collected in the hills above Clapham. The Orchid Cyprepedium calceolus and 'Birds Eye Primrose', Primula farinosa, are two which are described in glowing terms.

Valleys, woodland, limestone gylls leading to the open moors and, dominating it all, Farrer's beloved Ingleborough, fed and nurtured his interests—exploration, painting, botany and plant hunting. At fourteen Farrer began building his first rock garden, combining this with a pool and bog garden for moisture loving plants; his interest in botany was not confined to Alpines. Indeed, this becomes increasingly obvious to anyone reading his books or the list of plants Farrer introduced to cultivation.

After leaving Oxford he travelled extensively in the European mountains. He climbed to remote colles and over tumbling scree slopes searching for plants to either collect, paint, or just make notes on; learning in fact the practical details of a professional botanist and plant hunter. For unlike the majority of plant hunters, who served a long apprenticeship in a nursery, private or botanic garden, Farrer acquired his knowledge almost as a dilettante, in the sense that it was never an essential part of earning his living. Self-imposed discipline, inspired by a deep and abiding interest, produced a man who wove his own vivid contribution into the rich tapestry which records the history of botanical explorer/plant hunters.

In his books Farrer reveals a love of plants, plants that he describes at times in such extravagant terms that it is almost as if Eden had been rediscovered. In the Dolomites his genius was given opportunity to blossom. The portrayals of scenery come closer to capturing the essence of this loveliest of mountain ranges than any I have read. Farrer's pen paints pictures of flowers almost as precise as colour photography, and brings the plants described vivaciously to life.

The towns, villages and, particularly, the hotels have changed since the book was first published in 1913. Access to centres of interest is easier and, thanks to modern transport, quicker and more comfortable than in Farrer's day. The mountains, and the plants which grow upon the meadows, moraines and arêtes which collectively form 'King Laurin's Garden' are unchanged; Phyteuma comosum still cannot be reached without rope and piton.

For me, as it was with Farrer, Eritrichium nanum remains, indisputably, the King of one's Alpine experience. Though, unlike Farrer, my introduction to those unforgetable azure Forget-me-not flowers came on a day that was touched with all the gentle loveliness of spring as it finds expression on the Pordoi and Angstbord. To be amongst the hills is the supreme pleasure, but to be taken there in imagination through the pages of a book written by the hand of a master is a quite excellent substitute for the reality.

GEOFFREY SMITH
1985

CONTENTS

CONTENTS

THE DOLOMITES

CHAPTER I

THE GARDEN GATE

KING LAURIN'S GARDEN is a land of magic, enclosed
by peaks like frozen flames. It was long held an
impenetrable and enchanted country: mystery surrounded it, and the splendid terror of its pinnacles.
Old faiths had their refuge in the unhistoried tran-
quillity of its secret places, and even when the
unsatisfied emotions of the nineteenth century
began veering more and more eagerly to mountains,
more and more stimulating in their sympathetic
austerity, it was many years before the traveller
dared to turn his steps into wildernesses so
mysterious. Switzerland had been for several
generations the tennis-court of our suburbs before
an audacious maiden lady at last decided to embark
upon a tour in those inhospitable ranges. And
when at last she did so, we who are going to travel

thither in high comfort may well marvel to read of
her courage and hardships and exploits, solemn and
stirring to relate, as if she were venturing indeed
through the darkest tangles of Africa.

King Laurin's Garden is called " the Dolomites "
to-day, and the King is gone. Perhaps he lingers
secretly still in his Rose Garden up above the
Antermoja Lake, but I have never met him there,
and his roses are no longer to be found amid the
greyness of that desolation. And the barriers of
mountain have proved false, and yearly floods of
trespassers flow in and champ their mayonnaise
of chicken in fat hotels beneath the walls of the very
Marmolata herself. But of those hordes too small
a percentage, even now, is English. And since
the wonderland of Europe is open to-day to the
traveller, I am embarking on this book in the hopes
of tempting thither yet more and more of my
fellow-countrymen.

I see no reason whatever for being churlish, nor
will I adopt the conventional affectation of lament
for wonderful hills and valleys laid open to Tom,
Dick, and Harry. I am Tom and Dick and Harry
myself; there is in me no superiority of austerity or
endurance, and I have no prejudice against comfort
and soft living. Indeed, I revolt against the haughty

pose that resents the intrusion of tourists on one's
own mountains. "One's own," indeed! How can
they be one's own, unless through one's appreciation? And is the pedestrian peak-bagger, then,
the only one who can appreciate? And can anyone
seriously say that appreciation is dulled by comfort,
and that the Drei Zinnen are less glorious from a
comfortable loggia after a good dinner, than from
a soaked hay-bed, through the rifts of some gaping
cow-hut in a snow-storm, after a hunch of black
bread and a piece of cheese?

The superior tone of those who lament the
vulgarization of the mountains is pure egoism;
nothing more nor less. I know that feeling well
myself; far, far sooner would one have one's pet
peak or pass uncontaminated with the presence of
other malignant emmets like oneself. So far, good;
the sentiment is mere human sense. But it is
intolerably characteristic of our humanity to go
on and drape its selfishness in the tinsel of noble
fustian about the undefiled mountain solitudes—
which are never defiled by one's own presence,
forsooth, but always and only by that of other
people, with their sisters and their cousins and
their aunts. Such fine feelings as this do not bear
inspection for a moment. And how can mountains

be vulgarized? Vulgarity begins at home, in the
vulgar, and can live nowhere else. The more
people go to the mountains, the better for the
people, and no worse for the mountains. The
crassest chicken-champer must certainly derive more
good from meals beneath the Schlern or the Great
Vernel than if he sits stuffily over sausages in
Hamburg or Harrogate. I cannot believe that the
veriest tripper can go home again without some
grain of benefit, however small, from the wonderful
things amid which he has been moving, apparently
unseeing, in motor-cars and chars-à-banc. For in
the stupidest and most perfunctory word of admira-
tion launched between two courses, there lives the
germ of some happiness hereafter, some blurred
remembrance at a desk or an office stool, some
sudden breath of mountain air at the corner of a
street.

Thus, at least, I know it is with me. And so
I believe it therefore is with all. Accordingly,
however keenly my own selfishness may resent a
crowded picnic on the Forcella Lungieres or the
ridge of Rocca Longa, I will firmly recognize that
this *is* mere selfishness, and nothing nobler. When
all the tourists have come and fed, and prowled, and
gone again, there will always, after all, remain a

hundred thousand nooks and corners among the hills to which their feet will never care to ascend. Let us fly ourselves, if we will, to these; and meanwhile let us ungrudgingly concede them the many beauties and comforts that they appreciate—the very fact of liking them and wanting them is the beginning of salvation. As for higher flights, it is a deplorable rule of life that the better things can only be attained with effort, and the very best things with most. There will still be many famous peaks without funiculars; the tourist will make for these, the austere tourist will hurry into uncontaminated districts; as for me, I shall certainly always go up in whatever funiculars there are, and leave the genuine mountaineer to curl his lip at me in a contempt which I will neither feel nor assume towards weaker vessels than myself.

So I am going to make public prey of my joy in the Dolomites. Indeed, these strange mountains have a fascination beyond all other ranges. I was gloomy and reluctant, I remember, on my first visit to them, many years ago. I have a passion (which I am told is vulgar) for vast mountains and ice and snow; a mere 11,000 feet made me sniff. Had I not come straight from the twelves and fourteens of the Ortler and the Bernina, clothed in glistering cliffs of snow and ice? I arrived, cool at heart, prepared to criticize and cavil; and I went through the Dolomites as a pig through a sausage-machine. They made pounded mincemeat of me, rolled me out, smashed my snobberies flat, and dismissed me at the end their insatiable worshipper. Or perhaps it was the spell of King Laurin laid upon me. In any case, year by year I am drawn to them again more and more irresistibly. Each season, wherever I may be, I find myself discovering fresh reasons for having another look in upon the Dolomites. I have now got to such a pitch that I am quite capable of taking Misurina as a convenient half-way house between London and Brighton; and a forth-coming expedition to the Pyrenees which I have long been planning only remains obscure to me because I have not yet got a sufficiently plausible excuse for having lunch at Bozen on my way. Perhaps Heaven will send me an aunt in Vienna; in which case family piety will triumph with an ease unknown before.

I cannot escape the charm of the Dolomites; but perhaps it will assuage me a little if I try to share it with others. Their call is worst in these dark declensions of the year, when clouds and gloom and rottenness rule the garden; yet no less potently it comes again in June, when London is afloat in that mysterious fragrance of warm lilac (even where no lilac is) that makes the wonder and charm of Town in moonlit nights of early summer. Then indeed am I gripped suddenly by the throat one day with a longing to be away in the clean silence, amid the dancing glory of the Pordoi or the Belvedere. Baedeker beckons to me from his corner of the shelf, and I begin feverishly to ponder what possible purchaser I can find for my soul that my release may be brought about. Not that I would have you think I seek satanic assistance; the soul-purchasers of to-day are publishers. Their terms are much lower than those of their prototype; but their exactions, on the other hand, are smaller.

Here, then, I am vending a substantial slice of my inmost being, measuring you out my happiness in lengths of many thousand words. I cannot pretend that the transaction is sordid. At the risk of cheapening my soul in the market, I will confess that I know few pleasures keener than that of thus offering people the chance of sharing mine. I know and hear of so many who have followed on my tracks among the hills, and found there the same peace and ecstasy as I; and I know, too, that I am safely addressing only those chosen who will

appreciate what I have to tell them. Those who
dislike mountains and are bored with plants need
have no dealings with this volume. And meanwhile I will go ahead serenely, diffusing joy among
those who share it, and incidentally invoking sunshine and rapture on my own behalf, and glittering
mountain air over banks of flowers, to tide me
through the grey long winter when all my garden
lies sere and sodden and sombre under a shroud of
dead, rotting leaves, till even the eye of faith
becomes ophthalmic in the strain of trying to find
something there to see.

In this book though, I am holding out the hand
of my company, not only to my gardening friends,
but to all those also who love the hills in general,
but know nothing special of their flowers, and are
content to look upon *Primula vulgaris*, not as a
perennial, acaulescent, dicotyledonous herb with
revolute vernation, but as a mere primrose by the
river's brim. Therefore, while giving still what
help and information I can to gardeners, I shall
peptonize and compress it, that it may not bulk so
large as to prove unpalatable to the outside world,
nor make too heavy a demand upon the athletic
power of skippers. And, on the other hand, I
hope that my pages may be found a little fruitful

also in general information for the intending traveller.

The Dolomites are popular in people's mouths, but apparently the general stream of English emigration has not yet fully set in their direction. To judge, indeed, by literature and conversations at dinner, one would imagine that this district was a sort of annexe to Hyde Park. Can it be, though, that the more authoritatively people talk of places, the less they have been there or intend to go? Does the English polite *Sommerfrischler* talk at loud large about the Dolomites, and then shelter his frugal holiday at Ilfracombe? These are dark wonderings; my innocence would never have conceived such a thought if it were not that often as I have been in the Dolomites, at every season, crowded or empty, I have never found my countrymen in anything but a microscopic minority. In high summer one year I did not once hear my own language until I arrived at Cortina; and Cortina is a place apart, not to be ranked as belonging to the Dolomites. It is a succursal of the Athenæum, and is thicker than Bel-alp with Bishops. For the rest of the district, you may gauge the sparseness of the English from the fact that hotel chaplains are rarer a great deal than *Primula Juribella;* while the

itinerant old maid (*Femina vastatrix*) has woven
over this country as yet no such blight of Utrecht
velvet and German waiters as, in her locust-like
descents, she has shed so densely over Grindelwald,
Murren, and Trafoi.   Therefore it may be taken
that, for all their brave words and pretty picture-
books, not nearly enough English people go for
their soul's health to the Dolomites.   This lack
shall now be remedied.   I appeal from the " populus
male informatus ad populum melius informandum."

To do this, it is essential to give information.
The Dolomites form a rough square upon the map
of Europe.   Those blank, bald spaces with which
one beguiles one's fancy at railway-stations, wonder-
ing over blobs connected by straight lines, like some
bacterial diagram of a disease, give one no notion
that between the blobs called Innsbruck, Lienz,
Belluno, Verona, is contained a paradise of mountains more wonderful than anything in a Chinese
dream.   On the north runs the deep valley of the
Drave, the dun-coloured dulness of the Pusterthal ;
from this at right angles descends into the laughing
south the roaring Eisak in gorges of crimson
porphyry, and through wide vinelands, blue and
golden, fragrant in June as nothing else on earth.
The southern boundary of the square is the line of

the Lombard Plain where the mountains die
suddenly away, and from some summit you can
just see, far up in the north, the great dome of the
Marmolata, looking like a glistening soap-bubble
over the intervening ranges. And the last and
weakest side of the square is the valley of the
Piave on the east.

There are three main entrances to the Dolomites.
One from Venice and Belluno up to Cortina or
Caprile presupposes that you are already at
Venice. The others are more *praktisch* from
the point of view of the intending traveller. You
can enter the Dolomites from Bozen in the Adige
Valley on the west. Or you can enter them from
the Pusterthal by Toblach on the north. But
there are dietetic reasons why Bozen should be
taken last. And there can be no question that on
all counts the nearest and most convenient entrance to the heart of the range is from Toblach in
the Pusterthal.

You leave London at eleven in the morning of
one day, and you are at Bâle about six of the next.
And here comes in the one reason why it is that
we too seldom fare so far afield as the Eastern
Alps. For they are certainly farther away than
Switzerland, and the journey is both longer and

more expensive. Not so very much though, and
not at all by comparison with the advantages
gained. Granted, then, that by three o'clock of
the next day one has safely arrived from Bâle in
Grindelwald or Rosenlaui, so, by three o'clock,
too, from Bâle, one is arriving in Innsbruck. And
who will find hardship about spending the night
in Innsbruck? Indeed, I should rather call it
a privilege, so charming is the dead imperial city,
sitting deep beneath its mountains by the muddy
tide of the Inn. At every street's end there is a
view of stern and snowy peaks impending. When
the evening comes is the moment to see the Hof
Kapelle, the essential glory of Innsbruck. Here,
in a tiny, dingy little church filled with eighteenth-
century Jesuitries and monuments to the inevitable
Andreas Hofer, is packed the gorgeous tomb of
the Emperor Maximilian. In the centre is a great
box-shaped edifice of marble, carved in exquisite
and elaborate scenes from the Emperor's life. You
see him marrying Mary of Burgundy; you see him
interviewing the Borgia Pope, attacking cities and
receiving their submission; you see him holding
friendly intercourse with an elegant, bearded youth,
who turns out to be Henry VIII. The whole is
enclosed in a railing of gilded bronze; and on the

casket lid, his train flowing out behind, kneels the Emperor, robed and crowned Augustus, with Four Cardinal Virtues attendant on the corners. The whole work, as planned and as executed, is exactly representative of Maximilian, that engaging and ineffective scoundrel, always grandiose in promise, always futile in performance. Flanking the casket on either side stand colossal bronze figures of the Emperor's more desirable family connections and ancestors. These are for the most part vastly, pompously, supremely bad—bad with the riotous and stolid ornateness of the German Renaissance. They are Kings and Paladins and Emperors, helmed and crowned, cased in armour of bronze filigree like objects from some brazen wedding-cake, or trailing imperial robes all figured on their metallic surface with eagles and rich devices. Some are allowed no faces, but wear huge beaked helmets like nightmare birds, crested ferociously. There are bland, bun-faced ladies, too—Mary of Burgundy, Bianca of Milan, Juana la Loca—leaning about in Düreresque curves, and languidly lifting the folds of their ample vestments. And all these, aligned at fair intervals down some huge and splendid aisle, would make a general effect both imposing and splendid. Huddled up as they here are, in a dense line, and in far too small a church to hold them, they have more the effect of a queue at a booking-office. Even so there has not been room for all of them, and four have been crowded out upon the chancel-steps.

And yet—and yet, if you go into the dingy, dark little church at twilight, those colossal figures, dimly seen, have a certain awe. In the left-hand side especially, as you look up, the heads and poses are so arranged that the whole line looks as if engaged in animated conversation. I have a particular feeling for the most gorgeous of them all— Maximilian's father, the Emperor Frederick, with his worn and foxy old face. The two good figures, however, produced by Peter Fischer of Nürnberg, are on the other line. Among the carthorse-like proportions of the rest these have a strange and almost feeble grace of poise and limb. Arthur of England is singularly beautiful though ; not even his ceaseless reproduction on postcards and ink-stands can destroy one's feeling for the delicate manliness of his attitude, the quiet richness of his adornments, and his general air of well-bred and genial serenity. Theodoric, however, is made rather a nincompoop ; he stands with a weary and affected droop, like some posing woman on the stage. His artful curves are just those which were so dear to the sentimentality of the generations which admired the Belvedere Apollo, and went into glutinous ecstasies over the "modesty" of the Venus de Medici. And after him the line again tails off into monstrosities vaster and cruder almost than the rest. So much for the tomb of the last Cæsar who followed Justinian and Theodora in wanting seriously to be Pope as well. Grandiosely thought, peddlingly carried out, the grave of the Emperor answers exquisitely to his life of vain dreams, treacheries, and idle splendid flourishes. And for a last crowning irony—the Emperor is not buried here at all. The tomb is a cenotaph, and Maximilian lies obscurely at Wiener Neustadt, in country much more effectively illustrious nowadays, for the neighbourhood of *Dianthus alpinus.*

Next day you start again early over the Brenner. Indeed, if you choose, you can hurry straight through without staying at Innsbruck, and arrive at Toblach some time in the evening of the day after you left London. If I did not so delight in that glimpse of Innsbruck, with the peak of the Habicht towering close at hand, I myself would always do this. For, in truth, I do not love the Brenner, and should be glad to pass it in the dark.

It is the oldest in use and the lowest of the great Alpine passes. But I cannot rouse myself to any emotion over even its most dramatic moment, when the old Emperor Charles V., at the end of a life apparently triumphant, suddenly found his work toppling in ruins, and had to fly for his very freedom, only just in time to escape the clutch of Maurice of Saxony. Over the Brenner he precipitately fled (after an abortive attempt to get away from Innsbruck disguised as an elderly lady), and I have often tried to beguile the dulness of the pass with suitable emotions accordingly. None will come, and no amount of experience will ever make me feel that the Brenner is anything but a dull, green grove. Twice have I stayed there, and strayed through rain over dense lawns of the Fairy Primula high upon the Kraxenträger. But the general poverty of the flora in this district is grievous; and the mountains themselves are granitic, and, for the most part, of uninteresting lines. Look out, however, as you pass Steinach in Tyrol, for there you have a beautiful glimpse up to the right into a valley closed by peaks of weird and splendid shapes; and then again, as you descend the loop that comes down upon Gossensass, there is a magnificent sight of the glen leading up to the pyramids and snowfields of the Pflerscher Tribulaun. Otherwise the sooner you have done with the Brenner, the better you will be pleased. At Franzensfeste there is a fort, and you change (and in summer eat the best raspberry ices in the world), while your original train goes on southward to Bozen and Verona. As for you, you take the Pusterthal railway, diverging to the left at a right angle, by which you are soon deposited at Toblach.

Toblach is an ugly place in an ugly valley. The only Toblach with which the traveller need concern himself is the Toblach of the many hotels that line the square of green by the railway-station. Close behind them to the south rise high and steep, but ragged and shapeless, mountains, and at one point there is obviously a channel up into their fastnesses. But there is little beauty here, nor promise of it, to tell you that this is the northern gate of the Dolomites; that that channel is the road leading straight into their heart; and that all those huge hotels that look as if they were built of white or chocolate-coloured cardboard, exist solely to dismiss you comfortably upon that enchanted way. I have never really liked any of the hotels in Toblach; but that is merely because one only comes to Toblach to get away from it again as

soon as one can into the Dolomites. At the same
time, I must say a good word for the figs that are
here to be purchased in August. For some in-
scrutable reason they are sweeter and better than
any I have ever eaten in Bozen, Athens, Smyrna,
or Constantinople. At the same time, remember
that the hotels are far too polished and highly
civilized to provide you with such a plebeian fruit.
In all civilized centres of travel the dessert will be
found always to consist of wizened apples and
peaches green as young love and harder than
bullets. You have to go out and purchase figs for
yourself from the stalls in the open street.

It is from the Hotel Germania that the motors
start. For learn that the straight road into the hills
is called the Dolomitenstrasse, and that big public
motors, grey as destroyers and swift as smoke,
whirl their clients round to Cortina in a couple of
hours or so, and thence again through the utmost
wonders of the district, over the Falzarego Pass
and over the Pordoi Pass, and down the Fassathal, and over by Cavalese, and so up the valley
of the Adige again to Bozen. Our time, however,
for these magnificent conveniences in my judg-
ment is not yet. The drive to Schluderbach is
too brief and too beautiful for it to be necessary

to save hours of labour, as one must do to cross
the great passes. Also, I always go straight up
from Toblach to Misurina ; and because Misurina
happens to be just across the frontier in Italy,
the road thither, which diverges from the Dolomitenstrasse at Schluderbach, is so steep and so
dreadful as to be beyond the powers of almost any
motor (and, anyhow, they are forbidden). Therefore I usually charter a carriage, and drive at my
leisure. If one starts about ten, one is quite
happily at Misurina in time for lunch ; or one may
spend a lazy morning, and drive up in time for tea
or dinner, so short are the distances that inter-
vene between the dulness of the Pusterthal and
the splendours of the Dolomites.

CHAPTER II

FROM the first that drive is entrancing. The road, mounting imperceptibly, passes straight along the valley of the straight stream, clear as beryls, that comes down from the enclosing hills. On either side rise steep slopes of larch and pine; the morning air is solemn and scented; dew still dances against the sun on grass and flowers. One passes little lakes of a keen and thrilling green, and on the left a huge mountain-peak hangs over the road. In a little while, though, it sinks in one's eyes, for beyond, at the head of the view, comes into sight the huge tumbling castle of rock and ice which is the mass of Cristallo, Cristallino, and Popena. Cristallo, from the Dürren See, the second little green lake, looms upon one as something brutal and appalling. After the decent dulness of the Pusterthal, the sameness of the Brenner, one wants to be broken more gradually to earth's magnificent possibilities in the way of mountains.

20

It is true that on the way out, on leaving Zurich,
one had had a far panorama of the main Alps
resplendent in snow. But here one comes so
quickly to such close quarters; in a little while
Cristallo fills the sky, and his bulk is almost
terrifying. This view of him, too, is more colossal
than composedly beautiful; it is the huge and
hulking back-view of a giant. Cristallo turns
his noble company-face towards Cortina; upon
Schluderbach he casts out his glacier. Never were
the back premises of a mountain more obviously
his back premises, and even the rarity of glaciers
in the Dolomites cannot make this view of
Cristallo more dignified, or otherwise dignified
than by the large mass and castellated aspect of
the pile. For Cristallo ranks, indeed, high
among the great peaks of the district, although
its 10,495 feet are not especially difficult to achieve.

As you pass the Dürren See, look to your right
into a little strip of water on the other side of the
road, which here, but for the view in front, is flat
and dusty. This water is more keenly and richly
green than any other I know. It has an even
richer and much sharper note than Crême de
menthe, and always gives me special pleasure as I
pass. But it is possible that your attention will be

impossible to claim at this point, for before you
get to Landro, with its straight street and
trumpery-looking buildings, there opens up to
the left a deep gorge between sheer walls of
Dolomite. Into the heart of naked mountains it
runs, and their tops are flat and smooth as if made
on purpose to serve as a pedestal. For there
above them, at the head of that valley, in the
narrow vista between the cliffs, go soaring sheer to
heaven the peaks of the Drei Zinnen. From this
point of view the three Zinns seem three vast
pointed towers ; they are seen end on, in a great
wall, and shooting upwards from their pedestal
with the violent thrust of angry and immortal
tusks. On this northern side they fall away in
precipices like the side of a higher house than man
has ever raised ; clouds often wind themselves
between their cusps like soft, white dragons, and
their roseate walls are washed with those great
stains of black that are characteristic of Dolomite,
but specially conspicuous on the Drei Zinnen.
Look well and quickly while you may ; in another
moment stupid old Monte Piano wipes out that
valley, and the Drei Zinnen retreat for a while
from your sight.

Not that Monte Piano, from this point, is any-

thing but a very imposing and dominating force.
It looks impregnably lofty, yet up its sides run
little military zigzags, that often seem to end
nowhere in particular. All this valley is the play-
thing of the military. No photographs or views
are permitted ; and one passes watch-houses and
fortresses webbed in with barbed wire, from which
suspicious eyes are turned upon the traveller. The
eccentricities of frontiers are unforetellable ; if he
likes to avoid Misurina, the tourist can wander
through all the Dolomites without setting foot out
of Austria. But the Italian frontier traverses the
snowfield of the Marmolata, cuts off Civetta and
Pelmo, comes round across Sorapiss, and then,
with a wild bend, sweeps back to include Misurina.
Indeed, I have a theory that frontiers mysteriously
curl themselves about for my special undoing. In
all the districts where I want to go, and where my
most special plants are to be found, I am certain,
sooner or later, to find myself upon a frontier,
being pestered by suspicious Colonels, who cannot
be made to believe that any sane mortal would
visit Magiassone or Mont Cenis merely for the
sake of such coloured weeds as they may show.
However, as the Dolomite district by now is a
tourist country, no difficulties or discourtesy need

be feared anywhere upon the frontier, the more especially as our own nation enjoys particular favour, I think, in the eyes of both Italian and Austrian officials. In any case, the beaten track of the big motor-passes lies wholly in Austria ; but I must also add that wherever I have been, in corners no matter how remote and untrodden, I myself have never met with anything at the hands of the authorities but the most perfect courtesy and pleasantness, even when their duties compelled them to ransack the plants in my collecting-tin to make certain that they did not cunningly conceal photographs of fortresses.

At this point of the drive your attention is quite diverted from Monte Piano's bluff impending precipices ; for the main valley swerves suddenly to the right at Schluderbach, and there comes at once into sight above it the stark and perfect pinnacle of Croda Rossa. I have never been any nearer to the Croda ; almost any other view might spoil its lines, which from here are flawless, sweeping up into a huge pyramid of naked rock, above the long fall of its shingle slopes flowing away to the pine-woods far beneath. And Croda Rossa, too, has wonderful colour to match its wonderful shape. It is of Dolomitic rose and grey, filmed with blue veils where detritus has lodged on the ledges, and stained with those dark splashes that have already appeared on the Drei Zinnen. But near its summit it carries also a huge splash of scarlet, which, where the débris has fallen away, upon the snow and the shingle slopes has the very look of bright and rusty blood.

For the view of Croda Rossa alone it might be worth one's while to stay at Schluderbach. However, I have not yet done so; all the hotels have that gimcrack look that I have already noticed at Toblach, and the place does not allure me. If one is going up to Misurina, one goes on; if one is going on to Cortina, all the more does one go on. One thing alone might tempt me to linger in Schluderbach, and for even this it is as convenient and more pleasant just to stroll down from Misurina; for all these woods are rosy in the spring with the fragrant loveliness of *Daphne Cneorum*. Of this I never had any previous suspicion in former years, for, though people had talked to me of the pink Daphne down this valley, I had always taken it for granted that it must be the dowdy and universal *D. striata*, which is such a weariness to one's soul as soon as one has crossed into the zone of its distribution, which begins, so far as I have known it, in the Engadine. *D. striata* is universal throughout the limestones and granites of the Southern and Eastern Alps, while *D. Cneorum* is of much more limited distribution. Until last year I had only known it on the high turf of Monte Baldo, its heads of pink trumpets glowing amid the long grass of the mountain-side ; and then in June for the first time I came through the Dolomites, and there was the rosy loveliness of the Daphne scenting the whole valley, and gleaming richly in the woods round Schluderbach.

Even here it is of local distribution ; cross the frontier stream, and begin ascending towards Misurina, *D. Cneorum* ceases suddenly and abso- lutely, and its place is taken by abundant masses of *D. striata*. This last I have never collected nor grown in all these years, unless by accident, as a stray in some clump of something else ; but as many people have suffered many things on account of *D. Cneorum*, which, unlike the sun, frequently condescends to smile upon the comparatively un- just, and wholly withholds the light of its coun- tenance from the horticulturally just (thriving often with riotous profusion where no trouble has been taken, and nobody knows enough to realize that it is a difficult plant ; while in the garden next door, where learned gardeners have long consulted its needs, and compounded exquisite soils, it utterly declines to survive at all), I will here record that in the Ampezzothal, as often as not, it is growing in naked limestone silt or moraine, with no admixture of soil whatever. Even in the wood, though its too rare surface-fibres run through a superficial two inches or so of forest soil, leaf-mould, and peat of copse-wood decay, its yard-long rat-tail of nude yellow tap-root runs down into stuff that is nothing better than fine white limestone débris. It is not, it stands to reason, a pleasant or easy plant to collect; but I hope in future to see what I can do with it as a limestone plant. (Monte Baldo, of course, is a mass of limestone, too.)

At Schluderbach, where, when you are coming back, is the Austrian Customs, the Dolomiten-strasse curls away sharp to the right under Croda Rossa, and round to Cortina by the broad popular way (Misurina is merely a bypath to Cortina). Our own road runs the other way, across a level of woodland that once must have been a shingle-slide, past various parti-coloured frontier posts, across a little river, and then straight up the mountain-side, it seems, under Monte Piano. No more *D. Cncorum;* it ceases at the river. Among *D. striata* we sternly

climb, while opposite, across the stream, the
stony desolations of the Popena River begin to
unfold beneath the looming shadow of the Popena
Peak.   Now it is a case of walking, so abruptly
mounts the road.   Up and up, till Monte Piano
begins to sink into her true proportions.   In a few
more minutes we are on the upper level, and the
ragged pinnacles, that have long since begun to
appear, now unfold in all the majesty of the
Cadinenspitze.   We are almost above the woodland, and our way goes circling a stretch of Yorkshire marshland a-blush with *Primula farinosa*.
Then, a turn in the road, a little dip, and we
are bowling along the shores of the Misurina
Lake.

Perhaps I love Misurina with an excessive passion.
I think this sometimes when I have got there;
never when I am wanting to go.   In many ways
it is nearer general perfection than any other place
I know among the high mountains.   At the same
time, its beauties are not to be properly appreciated
as one drives along its shore from Schluderbach;
for it is along the bare right-hand side of the lake
that one drives, and the landscape at its farther end
in front is almost blocked out by a barrack-like
hotel, yellow and green, like a child's toy building,

adorned with faded scrolleries that add to its impression of cardboardishness. At its back the ground falls away steeply towards the Auronzo Valley far below, so that the only background one gets to that hotel is the tremendous and dramatic wall of all the Marmarole range, with Antelao and the soaring point of Sorapiss. Blue, soft in the clear air, and austerely splendid, they make the cruellest contrast possible to that ridiculously horrible erection in front, squatting so brazenly, all by itself, in the very middle of everything, just on the outlet of the lake. The other hotel crouches much more discreetly where the highroad dips upon the lake, but thus lacks the supreme glory of the view that (combined with its inner amenities) reconciles one so completely to the Grand Hotel Misurina as soon as one has passed its portals.

Between these two, all along the undulating shores of the lake, there stretched, when first I came to Misurina, a wide rolling lawn of grass and flowers, flowing down from the sparse pine-woods under the Popena ridge overhead; and in those far-off days (some five years since) that lawn was a-wave with sapphire bushes of the Willow Gentian, and starred with mats of Dryas and the orange fire of *Senecio abrotanifolius*. But all that beauty is gone by now, and hacked away. They are daily building more and more bald and hideous little houses on its site, and the Hotel Misurina (not the Grand Hotel) is here making itself a new offshoot (to be called the Hotel Sorapiss) to open in 1913, and, I am told, to combine the cordiality and comfort of the Grand Hotel with the more modest prices of its own parent.

None the less, I shall always, I hope, remain loyal to my first love, where my welcome is ever sure and my ways well known. I had a wonderful arrival there one spring, coming up by night from Cortina. It was after sunset that we started, and moonlight was full upon us by the time we got to Tre Croci. After this we drove through a weird silent world of half-lights in that dense forest, with great peaks, dim and ghostly, far above us against a sky of obscure sapphire. Dreamily we moved on through the moonlit dark of the woodland, and the Cadinenspitze overhead was like an enormous Peny-ghent, precipitous and misty pale upon the night, with the luminosity of snow-slopes falling from its lower face. At last we rose up into sight of the Grand Hotel Misurina, on the high level of the lake. And lo and behold! though our sulky driver had sworn that it would not be open for yet another fortnight, there it was, all lit up from end to end, as if a crowded feast were raging.   In the blue and silent darkness of midnight in the forest it was the strangest sight to see the blaze of all those illuminated rows of windows.   And when we arrived, I found that the hotel indeed *had* been shut, but that for me it had prematurely opened ; and for me was all that overpowering rehearsal of the electric light, which, as soon as I had been conveyed to bed, gently languished and died.

Therefore I lead you without qualm to the Grand Hotel ; nor need you ever, at my leading, fear being brought into those hotels of luxury and pomp which make the joy of sojourners in the Engadine or Oberland.   No one more loves nice eating and drinking than I do ; no one more detests that atmosphere which is called *luxe* or *luxus*—which stands for machine-made food, Utrecht velvet chairs, chamois horns, the *Daily Mail,* English old maids and chaplains, and vice-faced waiters in golden braid.   None such will you find with me, even when I bring you to palaces of ease like the Grand Hotel Misurina.   Here is clean freedom and comfort, and that simple pleasantness that you may expect of a house whose support rests, not on Germans from Hamburg, or English from the suburbs, but of the better-class Italian summer-freshers, come up for a long stay in the mountain-air from Venice or Bologna. Nor, indeed, will I ever lead you into squalor and the discomfort of dirt; but never, either, into the even more dismal discomfort of pretentiousness. Better an omelette of herbs in a small albergo than stalled insipid "rosbif" in a wide house.

There is little need to describe to you the view that greets your enraptured eyes when you emerge next morning into the glazed loggia that runs along the frontage of the Grand Hotel. I know nothing like it in the Alps; it is almost insolent in the compendiousness of its perfection. You have a picture of it, more lively than any that words of mine could paint. At dawn, at midday, at sunset, the Drei Zinnen have a splendour that varies perpetually, yet never grows less. There at the end of the view they rise, far above the lake, above the long descending folds of forest that flow from the lesser ranges on either side. Over the hotel on the right towers the long wall, which is all you can see from here of the Cadinenspitze; on the left rises the abrupt rampart wall of the Popena ridge, running up to the huge domed tower of Popena, with the mass of Cristallo behind. And out of

your back windows you have the panorama of
Marmarole, and the grim magnificence of Sorapiss.

But always it is the view in front, over the lake
to the Drei Zinnen, that holds one captive. The
lines of the shore are perfect on the woodland side,
curling into bays as cunningly proportioned as if
some master-gardener of Tang or Sung had made
the picture : at the precise point required there
rises the precise mossy boulder, or clump of Rhododendron, or tall fir-tree. One can scarcely believe
the picture to be natural. When first I saw the
place it was flawless ; there was even an island of
the right shape, with the right trees in their right
places. Next time I came, however, the trees were
dead ; and now the island is a horrid little flat
bean-shaped grass-plot, with a *Verschönerung* in
the middle, in the form of a peaked tin summer-
house, most dreadful to behold. And at the far
end of the lake, too, on a conspicuous knob, somebody has planted a villa-châlet like something out
of a toy-box. But these are specks on the sun.
For long days one could be happy here, sitting and
looking at the Drei Zinnen alone.

I do not approve of people who write travel-
books and insert huge slabs of other people's
writings in inverted commas. It is a mean way

of saving trouble, and cheating the publisher on one's tale of words. From one's own works, however, it is fair to quote; for, when one has done one's utmost best on any topic, it would be vain to improve, and silly to seek new words. (Thus Voltaire frankly takes a line from Corneille, who in turn had taken it straight from Sophokles; saying that when once the best thing had been best said, it could not be further bettered.) So I will use a previous description of the Drei Zinnen at sunset from a bygone novel of my own; not that I should claim that it is good, but I do not find how more fitly to express what I want to say. " In cold daylight the rock of them is peachy-pink, touched with russet, gold, and red: filmed in regular courses with a blue veil of lodged detritus, which is soft as the bloom on a plum. But at evening sometimes, as they tower in face of the sunset, with ranges of rose-red cloud above and behind, they become twin tongues of fire, blood-scarlet, terrible in their fierce and splendid incandescence. And as they flame unearthly, high above the unillumined woods, so in unearthly fires are they rendered again by the serene mirror of the lake, lying so clear and green and ghostly-pale in the dusk, luminous among the folded indistinguishable obscurities of the forest

round their feet." After all, I have rejewelled and
dejewelled this passage here and there, I find ; but
anyhow, it stands for what one may see the Drei
Zinnen do on some favourable evening of May or
September. For this is the special time for that
lobster-violence of evening colouring which is
echt-Dolomitisch, and even leaves the gaudy
and incredible picture-postcards ashamed of their
untruthful pallors.

I see that if I had my way I might spend the
whole of this book at Misurina. Come along, then ;
lest you feel defrauded ; I will take you for a few
expeditions round this place, and so pass on to
Cortina. First of all, for a lazy day before we take
to farther flights, nothing can be more delicious
than to browse about among the many paths that
thread the mossy pinewoods along the right-hand
shore of the lake. The forest is sometimes dense
and deep, and sometimes the trees stand sparse on
sun-dappled slopes where the banks are sweet with
Daphne striata, and odorous with the bees that are
always rifling it. Down by the pathside flicker
golden sparks of *Viola biflora*, and the Dainty Silene
sprays about in showers of white. The woodland,
too, is full of the Trefoil Anemone, exactly like our
own Windflower of the copses in springtime. But

here *Anemone trifolia* varies copiously into tones of soft and celestial blue among the Alpine *Pinguicula*, whose golden-throated bells are here as fat and fine as little snowy Gloxinias. Occasionally, in fallen boulders from the wall of the Cadinenspitze above, you will find *Saxifraga squarrosa* making close mats of grey lichen in the crevices; and on the open spaces of the woodland lie the fallen sapphire trumpets of the big Gentian, clustering in the deep moss of the glades, with tumbled stars over all the hummocks and tree-clumps of the purple Mountain Clematis. Pyrolas and other woodlanders abound; and rarely you may come on masses of Rhodo-thamnus, descended by chance from its proper ridges overhead, and sheeted with its wide, shallow saucers of soft pink. Indeed, the collector as a rule has little love for woodlands; but this forest by the lake at Misurina has especial wealth and charm. One might profitably wander alone in it for days; it is a place of sweetest fascination, alike for the gardener and for those who know not Daisy from Daphne, but are happy among beautiful crowded blossoms of a thousand colours, in the deep and delicious variations of a forest blue and green and violet in its depths, with glimpses of cerulean greys and pink flushes on the peaks beyond, half seen through branches from time to time.

CHAPTER III

AND ON TO CORTINA

AT first the practised gardener, I know, is apt to
cavil at my recommending Misurina with such
passion. And true it is to say that though the
whole valley is a galaxy of flowers, they are of the
commoner or more expected sorts, such as the
cultivator becomes hardened to after his first trip
into Switzerland. I know this snobbishness well
in myself : glorious as are the flowers of the central
chains in spectacular effect, they now bore me from
the gardening point of view. It is years since
I have been to Switzerland ; it may be I shall
never go again. Each season I desiderate further,
rarer, more secluded plants. I fly to more remote valleys each summer, of the eastern and
southern ranges, and suffer the penalty of increas-
ing experience in having to take three-day journeys
now for the sake of some one rarity away in Car-
niolic hills, where the language is like nothing

human, no word being of less than ten syllables, and these made up exclusively of *x*'s and *k*'s. Therefore, though the ordinary traveller will be wild with the ordinary joys of Misurina, I will now take you up on my favourite expedition, which is well calculated to satisfy even the most exacting gardener, to whom *Gentiana verna* is by now an un- heeded drug in the market. Collectors that I met one year at Misurina were at first a little critical of my suggestions that had brought them there. But I sent them up to the Forcella Lungieres, and they returned at last in a due state of contrite gratitude.

The Forcella Lungieres, the Drei Zinnen ridge of earlier allusions, is that spit of shingle which connects the mass of the Drei Zinnen with the last outlying spurs of the Cadinenspitze. You go along through the Misurina woods by Queen Margaret's charming walk. Colour-marks guide you all the way ; you cross a little marsh where the Bavarian Gentian shines like violent sap- phires, and then over open meadows, pink with the *Primula farinosa*. So you pass a stream and then up a steep, steep little climb to the Three Crosses of Rimbianco. The Three Crosses of Rimbianco stand upon a high knoll,

with a table and a bench for picnickers. All is
in bad repair; and of the Tre Croci only one
miserable relic survives. But one is glad to rest,
so magnificent is the backward view over the
towering splendours of the Cristallo mass, with
the rusty scarlet sword-point of Croda Rossa rising
over the flat summit of Monte Piano. Also, just
at the foot of this climb, there is a boulder all one
garden of Rhodothamnus, pink and delicate, and
on another block one's earliest sight of the Lovely
Potentilla hanging in a curtain of silver, starred
over with soft pale Dog-Roses.

After the Tre Croci the path turns round the
shoulder of the mountain and runs up into the wild
gorge that separates the Drei Zinnen from the
Cadinenspitze. It traverses great tumbles of rock
and fallen shingle from the wall overhead, and here
among the silt are the Saxifrages *cæsia* and *squarrosa* growing together abundantly in the fine-packed
stuff. A little farther along, in the shingle-tumbles,
lie the fragrant lilac tuffets of my beloved *Thlaspi
rotundifolium;* Rhodothamnus shines everywhere
among the bigger blocks or along their crevices,
while the wilder white stone desolations are
illuminated by the pale golden sparks of the
little Rhætian Poppy, so exquisite in its contrast

of large lemon-pale flowers, and blue-grey ferny foliage. So at last the glen comes to a blind end; and before you rises the last of your climb, the steep ridgy bank that surges up and up at the head of the valley, to form the connecting rib between the two mountain masses on right or left. One descends first into a tiny meadow not a hundred yards across, which is the last *plan* of the valley. And here, among the grass, for some reasons (I have rarely so seen it elsewhere) the Cushion Silene makes the field one blush of rich rose, through which in threads and blots and wide patches of pure colour go wandering the azures of *Gentiana verna*, with *G. bavarica* to follow.

Now the track goes climbing, climbing, climbing, toiling up over loose stone, and zigzagging among tufts of flowers. Behind us the prospect widens more and more; we are far above poor Monte Piano, and on our right the unsuspected spires of the Cadinenspitze open out. And on our left the Drei Zinnen fill the sky. We mount and mount towards their pedestal, and come at last into a paradise of flowers more beautiful than I can say. First the big Trumpet Gentian—in its duller *excisa* form, though—forms a carpet over the short, soft grass, pale still from the winter; and then, in a

little, the Fairy Primrose takes charge, veiling all
the hill in an undulation of soft pink.   And, after
that, marvel after marvel, while soft clouds hover
round the bastions of the Drei Zinnen, and behind
us, across the faces of Cristallo and the Croda, go
drifting long blue and lilac wraiths of storm and
snow.   So we climb still, over fields of Spring
Gentian, set with *Primula longiflora*, and arrive at
length upon the wind-swept crest of the ridge,
where the silted soil is washed into long ripples as
if by the waves of the sea.

The abruptness and glory of that sudden view
down into the Auronzo Valley on the other side of
the pass is something to take away one's breath (if
the wind does not do that), and make one forget
the dancing flowers for a moment.   Straight,
straight, and far falls the mountain-side, down
through deep slopes of woodland to the mapped-
out valley where the river runs like a tiny thread
of silver.   Along its banks in the distance, microscopic, lies Auronzo, and beyond, away into golden
Italy, float range after range of jagged mountains,
yielding at last to the plain far out beyond.   And
the colour on that wild day !   The bluest afternoon
of Ceylon has nothing to show more rich and soft
than the misty sapphire of those distances, and

overhead the sky was wonderful with masses of wild and racing cloud ; but above Italy hung serene heaven, luminous and golden-blue and calm as the sky of an Italian painter.

In face of us rises, across the unplumbed depths between us, the sheer wall of the Zwolfer-kofel, with its massive fortress-lines, and long ledges of russet and rose, with splashes of black, and filmed pale lines of detritus. And round to the left the path goes curving along the slopes of the Drei Zinnen and over the further levels of their pedestal. You may follow it, if you will, to the hut and the little hotel by the lake on their farther side. And away over the hills and among the Sexten Dolomites lies Pragser Wild See, down beside its gleaming water, in which the sunset renders the vast rosy wall of the See-kofel for the successful imitation of railway posters, the delight of painters, and the advertisement of its hotel.

However, for my own part, I have never stirred beyond the Forcella. The views, the flowers, the situation, are too absolutely filling. All the grass of the ridge is one lawn of the Fairy Primrose, its shilling-wide stars of pink lying in dense sheets flat upon the flat sheet of the plant; the ups and downs are rosy with it in a hundred shades. I shall never forget one little boss of grass that I came up to, against the light, out of a hollow. It was like shimmering pink silk. There were some thirty plants there, none less than two feet across, all in full flower, and growing so thickly that you did not dare to tread that turf of colour. And no two plants were in the same shade; their beauty ranged from palest to deepest rose. As one came up towards that spectacle, the flowers blended into one quivering sheet of colour, palpitating with its different tones. Then there are Auriculas of a specially valuable form—*P. A. ciliata*, small, powderless, with flowers of a very rich, deep golden yellow; and *Primula longiflora* growing all about among *minima* in the grass, looking like some gigantic, long-throated *farinosa*. As for the Gentians, never have I seen *verna* more magnificent and lavish—no, not even on the Mont Cenis—its azure stars forming deep splashes of colour on the banks. There lives a white form here, and a pale form, and a white *minima*, and every delightful luxury that you can want. And straight above you rises the black and rosy wall of the Great Zinn.

From the ridge you can hardly see that famous and deadly climber's pride, the Little Zinn; but

the Western Zinn and the Great Zinn are huger
masses, and of a magnificence overwhelming,
whether from near or far. But when you are
close up beneath them, you have an interesting
glimpse into the nature of Dolomite. From the
lake below, each peak looks as if it turned a perfectly plane face, with such perfect regularity are
the lines and ledges carried straight across each
pyramid. It is only when you are close that you
see each cone, in point of fact, not to be a solid
mass at all, but an enormous ragged mass of peaks
and pinnacles and buttresses one behind the other,
yet so regularly stratified that from a distance the
whole congregation of spikes and pinnacles looks
like one flat wall. Indeed, in the clear air of this
country, and with the glowing rose of the rock, it
is always very difficult in the Dolomites to make out
the true planes and relations of various towers and
cliffs; but I know no instance more conspicuous
and striking than this of the Drei Zinnen. From
the lake it looks as if any ascent must be along
the face of a sheer precipice. From the ridge you
can trace the route up the Great Zinn: It is a
series of scrambles up on to long traverses behind
balconies and bastions and pinnacles of outstanding
rock.

I know the ridge in many seasons and many moods. A little later all the Primulas and Gen_tians are gone, but in their stead are things more interesting, perhaps, though less brilliant in general show. Yet even this I dare not say when I remember that in August the silt of the ridge is cushioned with wide hassocks of *Potentilla nitida*, all a glow of richest rose upon its flat silver sheets. Then in the silt-pans not so very far away shine generous pearly moons of *Ranunculus parnassifolius*, specially to be noted as here being the form with magnificent round flowers, instead of the petalless fraud of the Piz Padella, or the wizened, twy-petalled abortion of the Monzonithal. Here it is glorious in wet, white, clayey silt, and shares its domain with the no less beautiful *R. Seguieri*, which is the limestone version of *R. glacialis*, but very different, with wide flowers of cleanest, glittering white, among fine, green, ferny foliage that develops from ramifying connected masses. Then there is the Monte Baldo Anemone, lavishing its white Chrysanthemums over the sunny débris slopes, and *Saxifraga cæsia* in a fine form, and Saussurea, woollily purple, and the mean yellow stars of *Ranunculus Thora* that succeed in being impressive by their abundance alone, and grey flannel Edelweiss, of course, in mats and masses all over the down. And then again, if you go up later still in the season, when everything but the Potentilla is gone, you will find that the little alpine Rhamnus which grows in tidy bushes over the rocks and ridges has turned to the most violent and terrible blood-crimson. In great gouts of pure fresh gore it bespatters the ridge, and the Sumachs of the Maritime Alps are by comparison dull and poor. But those autumnal glories sadden me, and the blood seems spilled from the sad wounded breast of Adonis, sinking gradually to his annual death. It is, I think, in June that the richest loveliness of the Forcella may best be seen ; but the ridge has not an empty moment between the going of the snows and their return.

Other expeditions pale beside this. But if you will, you may follow the road back towards Schluderbach, until the track diverges up the steep flank of Monte Piano through woodland, and thence under cliffs all starred with rosettes of powdery grey Auriculas with soft, golden heads of blossom. After a long, dullish toil you reach the flat summit of the mountain. Monte Piano is merely a view-point—a huge level undulation of lawns thick-set with flowers. But I, who ascended

it (on a hot day) because Baedeker says it has a
" rich flora " — forgetting that by a rich flora
Baedeker only means Gentians and common
Primulas, and such small, beautiful fry—was cross
because I found none of the rare wonders that I
craved, and consequently had but a jaundiced eye
for the famous view. Remarkably beautiful it is,
though, especially to the north and east, while
straight in front of you rises the flaming point of
Croda Rossa, with Cristallo to its left. But to the
north the prospect widens out over the far-off Pusterthal, and in the distance you see the granitic pyramids
about the Brenner, resplendent in gleaming snow.
Wonderful vast dolomite masses come next, and
in a gap between them, tiny and remote in the
north, the creamy cone of the Grossglockner.

And then to the right again, across the un-
fathomable gulf of the Schwarzer Rienz, tower the
Drei Zinnen, almost more powerful than ever, as
they stand foursquare upon their pedestal of rocky
level and shingle-slopes. From this point they are
seen end on, the Western Zinn so completely
dominating its rivals that the mass looks like some
cathedral of unearthly size, the Great Zinn and the
minor pinnacles all alike serving as the flying
buttresses and aisles to the enormous perfect tower

of the Western Zinn. So one sits outside the
Restaurant Hut, on the extreme edge whence
those fearful western precipices drop away towards
Schluderbach, and eats scrambled eggs and drinks
indifferent rough wine in face of a view well worth
the trouble—were it not, indeed, that almost any
walk in the Dolomites will give you views as
beautiful (though not perhaps so ostentatiously
panoramic), with the added advantage of spoils and
glories for the garden.

But, really, what do flowers matter in this
country? Every walk and every stroll is so
delightful and rewarding that it would be all pure
profit even if one saw nothing more horticulturally
stimulating than Groundsel by the way. It is only
because I have grown greedy that I can even
pretend to sniff at those many hours I spent on
Monte Piano. There were other tourists at the
Hut, and I by no means wished them away ; so
that I cannot have been wholly devoid of grace.
I remember how I returned, too, down an awesome
gully full of Potentilla and Saxifrage, and how I
got caught in a thunderstorm, and went to sleep
under a tree, and altogether had a perfectly arcadian
day. Another I had on the Col de Varda, which
is the jutting shoulder of crag which stands out

from the Cadinenspitze immediately above the
hotel. Here again there is nothing of any very
great interest, but the path goes delightfully up
among Gentians and Daphne and great white
Butterwort, until at last it emerges upon the high,
bare rock where Rhodothamnus is in sheets of pink,
and the Potentilla in sheets of rose and silver, and
the small Saxifrages sitting among the white stone
in tight little domes of grey. After this one
scrambles about among broken cliffs, with full
prospect over Marmarole, Antelao, and Cristallo ;
and so down again to the hotel in time for
lunch.

But even more to my heart is that fiercer zigzag
on the opposite side of the valley, which takes one
up to the Popena ridge in an hour or so. On its
crest there are just the same usual rock-plants that
you find on the Col de Varda, with *Phyteuma
comosum* totally ungettable in some of the precipices, and the Keltic Valerian, the true Spikenard,
here and there amid the stone-tumbles, perfuming
the wide air with its dowdy little sprays of blossom.
But the charm of this ridge lies in its view and
itself. When you reach the crest and see over, you
find yourself on a sort of double and treble little
fin-range of white rocks, and hollows in between

them filled with scented bushes. Among these you can lie your length in shelter, while the delicious keenness of the wind goes shrilling overhead, and in your eyes are all the glories of the earth ; in the south great peaks, Sorapiss, and further wonders far away across the Ampezzo Valley, and needle-like spurs standing out from Popena himself a little way farther on ; and in the north the creamy glistening snowfields of the Brenner, shining above the levels of Monte Piano. And over the edge you look down immediately into the gaunt upper valley of the Popena, from its source in the huge desolation of the mountain whose naked bulk towers so close above.

All this ridge is worn and weathered into the most fantastic pinnacles, big and little. In Italian these are "guglie"; according to my young brother, therefore, Julias, and when specially acute and terrible, " hairy Julias." The hairiest Julia of all is she who is called after Edmondo de Amicis. To see this you diverge along a lesser (labelled) track, just below the final ascent of the ridge, and come at last upon a thing like a factory chimney standing lonely, with the wall of the cliff at its back, and on the summit, top-heavily poised, a formation like some enormous decanter stopper. Edmondo's

Julia is, I believe, absolutely unclimbable—but the foot of man has been set upon her apex none the less. A rope was cast across from the mainland of precipice behind, Julia was lassoed, and bold mountaineers swarmed across that frail bridge on to her pinnacle. But this whole range is populous with Julias, though Edmondo's is their queen ; you can find them along the crest of sizes and degrees of hairiness to suit all tastes. I have had several happy afternoons among the Julias of the Popena ridge. They are perfectly Chinese in their wild shapes, and seen in mist (as in a charming sketch of Harry Rowntree's) their fantastic outlines, half revealed and half hinted, take one straight back to those weird landscapes of monstrous pinnacle and overhanging peak in which one had hitherto dared to disbelieve. But the Chinese painters of old knew what they were about; those mountains that they drew are Dolomite of the same form and wonder as these of the West.

Now, I am sure it is time to leave beloved Misurina; and though there are diligences and posts down to Cortina, the distance is so little, and may be taken so gradually, and the way is so wholly delicious throughout, that it may well be

taken on foot, baggage being despatched by some
convenient post. First one goes down a little, and
then, having passed the divergence where the road
descends and descends to Auronzo and Italy (for
here one is in the interregnal land), one continues
along the lower slopes of Cristallo, through the
most deep and dreamy pine-forest, losing sight by
mournful degrees of the Drei Zinnen (which are
never more overwhelming than when you first see
them suddenly, mounting from this side), and by
no means consoled with little sentry-boxes that tell
you you are now again in Austria. At one point
the road crosses a huge fan of desolation poured in
winter and spring from the riven ravelled flank of
Cristallo, now so immediately overhead in all his
naked magnificence that he looks as if any moment
we might share the fate of poor Maria Somebody
and her daughter Barbara, who were here caught
out of life by a stone that he let fall one day in
September—almost, to a day or two, the very
anniversary of my own last passing there—a solemn
coincidence which, like the birthday of Harriet
Smith, is really "so very odd." But after this the
road returns into the safety of the dense forest,
winds slowly upward again with increasingly
splendid views of the Sorapiss mass as one draws

closer, and ultimately comes to a luncheon-halt at
the huge and hospitable hotel which occupies the
Pass of Tre Croci, where there is a Customs'-station
for travellers coming from Misurina or Auronzo.
(The Italian station is Misurina itself.)

I cannot quite tell why Tre Croci is so fascinating.
I have often passed it, and always wanted to stay
there, and have never done so yet. It is, as I say,
a pass, a neck, between the woodlands that slope
down on either side from Cristallo and Sorapiss.
One most excellent expedition I know from Tre
Croci, which can be done from Misurina or Cortina,
and which I myself achieved one day from Misurina.
This is to take the path that skirts the northern
wall of Sorapiss (in which you will find *Primula
tyrolensis* impregnably ensconced), and then mounts
over a steep and precipitous shoulder into the high
glen which is, as it were, the backyard of Sorapiss,
filled with a rosy-grey desolation of stone-shingles
from an amphitheatre of peaks all round you overhead, with a clear little green lake in the middle.
Here there is the Pfalzgau Hut, kept in my time by
a charming old bearded Italian lady, with the figure
of an amiable elephant and the laugh of G. K.
Chesterton, who in a moment will whip you up
the oddest froth of batter that ever you met with

under the name of an omelette.   The flowers here
were disappointing—only Poppies and Thlaspi and
Anemone baldensis ; but the surroundings are their
own reward, so austere and noble.   Further, across
the Auronzo Valley, deep down below, one has a
sight of the Cadinenspitze as one had never known
them before.   From the Forcella Lungieres their
clustered needles are terrifying ; but from the
greater distance of the Pfalzgau Lake one can see
their whole composition, and how the group rises
from its plinth in a vast Milan-Cathedral-like composition of spires and minarets and campanili.   Or,
to take a better simile, like a certain fine colony
of stalactites that depends from a lone hollow
of the Ingleborough Cave, and can be seen
reflected in a pool, a very city of delicate aspiring
obelisks.

Otherwise I know nothing of Tre Croci, except
that I should like to know more.   For rarely does
one come upon a place more full of attraction.
The road down to Cortina, though, is surely one of
the worst in the world.   For Austria is disinclined
to make it easy for you to get up to Italy and
Misurina.   However, with the rapid growth of the
tourist trade, I think this attitude will be modified,
and we shall have yet another proof that there

is nothing like wholesale nomadry for binding humanity together, and making the nations realize at last that the tastes and interests of everyone are much the same after all, and dependent for their gratification (and the means of it) on mutual goodwill. On the other hand, the road down to Cortina is specially beautiful in the widening splendour of its views at every moment, as one descends towards the smiling breadth of the Ampezzo Valley, all meadows and pleasant open land, with the dome and masses of Tofana on the farther side, ruddy Pomagognon and Cristallo on your right as you come ; on the opposite side of the sky-line, Nuvolau, the Five Towers, the Croda da Lago, the Becco de Mezzodi, with the stupendous bulk of Pelmo peering over their shoulder, and seeming to make part of the range, although so far away beyond, across remoter valleys. To your left are the walls of the Faloria Alp above the woodland, and then the Wall of Malcora leading up towards Sorapiss. Down goes the road through sun-dappled woods of larch, and over flowery cushions of Dryas and *Dianthus monspessulanus,* fringy and sweet. Here and there are crosses to record the deaths of travellers whom the blizzards have caught and killed in winter on the pass, and

in autumn on the cliffs and rocks above the stream,
the dying leaves of the Keltic Valerian are bright,
pure gold among the darkening shrubs ; and the
lilac goblets of the Colchicum are thick in the fields.
So one comes down at last upon the civilization of
Cortina.

CHAPTER IV

AND AWAY AGAIN

LET others sing the praises of this lovely place and its innumerable expeditions. It is the centre of ease and comfort in the Dolomites, swarming nowadays with vast hotels, each more magnificent than the last, and endowed with bands, bric-à-brac shops, and every other refinement of polite luxury. Nothing, however, can spoil the native beauty of Cortina, lying as it does in the wide shallow valley of the Ampezzo, among green meadows, with a far-off fringe of deep pine forest, and then above this, farther yet, the high bare Alps and the great peaks, rosy and grey. This "farther yet," to my mind, is the damning fault of Cortina. It is really too far from the hills. For those who are tired or lazy, and only want mountains as an agreeable decoration to be looked at in the distance, Cortina is paradise. But to get up thence into the solemn and lonely places means an expedition hardly to be

achieved in the day. I have never yet been tired
or lazy enough to linger in Cortina ; I have never
yet had time to treat it as it deserves. For
Cortina should be made the centre of a long stay,
the base or skeleton for intervals of joy among
the mountain-huts. I should like to make it my
headquarters for a couple of months or so, taking
trips all the time of a week and more among the
refuge-huts of Tofana, Sorapiss, and the Croda
da Lago, and so forth.

Otherwise this is only a place for the elderly, or
idle, or broken, who like to be in to lunch, and have
a comfortable tea in an arbour, with picturesque
waiting-maids, clad in Tyrolese costume. These
are the essential fashions and charms of the Hotel
Faloria, perched up among the pinewoods under
Sorapiss. This famous house is especially frequented
by the English, and more especially still by English
Bishops. It is rarely that one cannot flush a brace
in the Faloria. And up behind the Faloria there
is a great russet cliff of adamantine hardness in
which the Phyteuma abounds, but cannot be
extracted by utmost skill of knife or trowel. As
for the milder expeditions round Cortina, they are
obviously legion. I will not chronicle them, never
having done anything in this region except pass

through as quickly as possible on my way to the
heights again. I will only add that in the parish
church lie the desiccated remains of SS. Liberalis
and Theophilus, whoever they may have been.
Their horrible atomies repose in glass coffins, done
up, faces and all—but it only makes the faces
worse—in swaddling bands of muslin, tight to the
shrunken ribs and pipe-stem twisted limbs, and set
with tags and tassels of tinsel, with glass jewels,
and dusty odds and ends of velvet. They are very
dreadful; it is surely not possible that any holy
thought or profit can linger round such spectacles.

I know of no other useful information that I can
give you about Cortina—none, at least, that I could
not cull from Baedeker, and which you, therefore,
may just as well look out for yourselves; so I will
now escort you away up to the Falzarego Pass,
only noting that if you wish to see the Agordo
Valleys, and make close acquaintance with Pelmo,
you must go a little way down the long road that
leads to Belluno, past S. Vito di Cadore, to Borca.
As for us, our place is now in the sumptuous
motor that twice daily, if not more often (and
there are subsidiary services to the Karer See),
grinds so easily up to the Falzarego, immediately
under the dome and southern wall of the Tofana di

Rozes. And oh the joy of being smoothly carried up an enormous mountain-side that otherwise one would have had to conquer with able and untiring, but unwilling, feet! There are few luxuries so keen as that of motoring in the mountains, and seeing the valleys sink swiftly into littleness beneath one's gaze, without one's having had to do a foot's turn to reach these heights. And then again, one rejoices no less in the other contrast, when one has sweated up some pathless, roadless steep, and reached some noble place unattainable by car or carriage, with every muscle rejoicing in the work it has done, and a glad heart triumphant over its many pantings on the way up, and a great, fine feeling of superiority over "carriage people." Most of one's joys are matter of contrast, indeed; and after hard days among the hills, I "snuggle," like a Maurice Hewlett heroine, into my cushioned stall in the motor.

So we are whirled up and up and up out of the Ampezzo Valley on the side opposite to that walk down from Tre Croci. The road is a wonder of engineering, curling here and there along the face of the mountain, and piercing through tunnels hewn in the hard limestone. As we rise, the view opens out behind, and Cristallo towers to new heights above Pomagognon. Then, below the unfolding magnificence of Sorapiss, gradually the new splendour of Antelao emerges, to rule the valley far down at his feet. Antelao is a noble mountain, and he rejoices in a glacier, which is a sort of Garter among the Dolomites ; his shape is that of a sweeping pyramid, towering up towards a peak of snow and ice. He dominates the picture as you mount towards the Falzarego Pass, and almost makes you forget to wonder what may be the names of certain pale blue spires, very fantastic and phantasmal, away down in the south towards Belluno. No doubt they are the Cadore Dolomites ; it is as morbid to be perpetually wanting to know the names of mountains as it is to ignore utterly the places you go to, and to let yourself be taken blindly hither and thither with no more interest than an umbrella.

I have had fierce arguments with the various people I have at times convoyed abroad. They one and all concur in never having any idea of where they are going, what they have seen, and how they got there. And this in spite of much preliminary poring over maps, and planning the delights of travel. And I, who certainly like being left to " boss " the tour, find, all the same, that

there comes a point at which acquiescence becomes
an insult to the contriving power. Too blank and
obstinate an apathy towards plans and places seems
to betray a lack of interest in the whole proceed-
ing, and one would even hail at last a little (evanescent) hint of criticism or opposition, as suggesting
at least some sign of life and "taking notice." The
cruellest of all companions are they who never care
to remember names ; for to me, who cannot fail to
associate a place with its name, and find the beauty
of a mountain mysteriously symbolized by the
beauty of its proprietary syllables, it is ridiculous
to pretend that you can adequately remember and
incorporate such and such a splendid peak if you
have no notion what it was called, nor how you
came to see it, nor when, nor where, nor why.
What does it help you to look in your diary and
read, " I saw a mountain " ? Their names are
parts of all beautiful things. I do not mean such
sham names as Mount Baker and Mount Cook and
Mount Bullock Workman, of course—these are not
names ; they are mere tags—but if a peak have
grown through centuries into the habit of being
Antelao, you can never properly retain its full
essence, or as much of it as your soul is big enough
to hold, unless you have at least so much elementary

interest in the thing as to remember where it was, and how called, and in what relation to other peaks.

It depresses me when my companions have no ideas as to where they are going or what they are seeing. Perhaps this is silly sentimentality on my part, but to me all the mountains that I care about are definite personalities, with features and characters and names that belong as exclusively to them as mine to me. The names of all my friends, human or alpine, are parts of them, and symbols of themselves that I accept and hold as such. I should not know the Marmolata if I suddenly tried to think of her as Rochemelon ; any more than I should know my own father under the name of Alexander or Lord Roberts. Not, of course, that one wants to burden oneself or one's readers with the name of every mountain that one sees, good, bad, or indifferent, any more than one loads one's memory with the name of every woman one meets at a garden-party. But there are outstanding individuals in all sorts of crowds ; and I do not think anyone is fit to come among the hills unless he has at least sufficient interest in beauty to differentiate between peaks and know them apart, and love those that are pre-eminent in beauty. And how is he to arrive at such differentiation unless he adopts the handy and simple symbolism of names? And if you merely take the mountains as a pretty panorama, then you are not fit to come among them. At least, you may be in slow process of becoming fit by the very fact of coming among them at all; but I had rather you did not come among them with me yet awhile.

Even so do the uninstructed love flowers as a mass of colour, a panorama of planting, natural or artificial; but the very first beginning of real interest makes it necessary to fix each specially beautiful kind with a name of some sort, though years may pass before you advance yet farther to the awful necessity of remembering botanical polysyllables. And one always remains eclectic in one's nomenclature. To this day there are a hundred hideous little umbellifers and composites even in the Alps, of which I myself neither know the names, nor want to. By so far does my own sympathy fall short of being catholic, or else I should have to know every name that ever came into my experience. As for the mountains, you cannot ride off on the weakness of your memory. It is only your close friends among the hills that you must have their clothing syllables for; and however weak your memory, do you find it so hard to remember the names of your cousins, and your aunts, and the Georgianas that you fall in love with? Believe me, your special mountains are fewer in number than they, and no less vivid in presentment—if, at least, you have soul enough to have any beloved mountains at all.

CHAPTER V

By now we are well up out of the Ampezzo Valley, and the wall of Tofana looks as if it might crash down upon us at any moment—a thousand feet of stark, rosy limestone, absolutely sheer above the road. Then as we rise above the forest towards the Alpine levels and sparser pines, there come out upon the sky-line to the left a cluster of square bulks like a shattered castle of great towers, toppling drunkenly this way and that. These are, indeed, the Five Towers, and beyond them, far higher and more august, there soars into view the almost ecclesiastical spire of the Croda da Lago. All these rise from the downs of naked limestone and stone-shingle, to which the pass does not attain; for, having wound close under the gaunt expanses on which stands the Nuvolao, our road comes to a halt at the Hotel Falzarego, in an amphibious sort of neck between one mountain-mass and the other, where there are fallen boulders, indeed, but also a few pines and grass.

Straight above rises the Cima Falzarego, and behind us now Tofana; and all these mountain wildernesses are set with hospitable huts, so that in summer one might spend a fortnight of deifying refreshment on each, wandering slowly from *Schutz-haus* to *Schutzhaus*, among the barren roseate valleys of shingle, filled with pure air and flowers and silence. The Sachsendank Hut sits by Nuvolao, the Wolf-Glanvell in the heart of Tofana, the Reichenberger on the shores of a little pine-girt green lake, close beneath the threatening spire of the Croda da Lago. And there are many more beyond counting, all of which you will find in Baedeker and in local maps. You have nothing to do but to go there, be welcomed, well fed, and given a comfortable room of four clean walls, a bed, a table, and a chair. Then you pay the ridiculously small bill that is asked of you at the end (and if you are a member of any Alpine club, that little becomes still less), and wander on your way rejoicing to the next. Obviously this is no life for luxurious women, nor for those who must always move with a multi-plicity of boxes; but for men who enjoy plain comfort there is no pleasure like this of these

Alpine huts so thickly scattered over all the high ranges of the Austrian Alps from the Ortler to the Obir. They open at varying times between the middle of June and the middle of July, and have a resident landlord thenceforth until the tourist season ends in September. I shall give you a more exhaustive sample of them in good time.

The Hotel Falzarego is not quite on the summit of the pass, unfortunately, or I should certainly go and stay there; but the Falzarego Hospiz, which does occupy the neck, has never tempted me. The view, however, as you begin to descend on the other side of the pass towards Pieve di Livinallongo, comes upon you like a douche of iced water and makes you gasp, as soon as you have got over the sorrow of saying farewell to Antelao and Sorapiss and Tofana. For suddenly, straight in front of you, over an unguessed profundity of mountain-range and deep blue valley, there stands the entire colossus of the Marmolata, Queen of all the Dolomites, though from here impressive only by dint of snowiness and vast bulk, rather than by the stern and awful beauty of her southern face. The Marmolata stands at the heart of the Dolomites, entangled in valleys; and, except from such a height

as this, is hard to get a sight of. She rises to nearly
11,000 feet (it used to be called 12,000 feet, and
more, in the days when Churchill and Miss Betham
Edwards had such ado to get a sight of her), and
has not only a glacier, but a very fine large glacier,
too. Her whole northern face is one snowfield,
upheld by huge cusps and bastions of rock, while
on the southern side she falls away in a sheer
precipice of 6,000 feet, which is among the most
terrifying magnificences in all the ranges of the
Alps. Imagine a very thick slice of melon laid
upon its side, and you will have a good bird's-eye
notion of the general shape and design of the
Marmolata, its plan, form, and effect; or else you
might think of it as a vast dead tooth stopped up
with snow. This is more its aspect from the passes
on the north—a bulk of unbelievable size and
volume, but not otherwise imposing, nor beautiful
in line.

Indeed, I often wonder helplessly in what even
the most perfectly genuine mountain-love can
ultimately be defined as consisting. It is quite
easy to go on one's knees before such obvious
glories as the Matterhorn, or the Viso, or the
Cimon della Pala. But what are one's real feelings
of joy among mountains that cannot honestly be

called beautiful at all? There are many such—
gaunt, shapeless huddles of rock, brutal, hostile,
and frightful. Only snobbish sentimentality could
deny this. And yet one is happy among them.
Perhaps a generation or two ago their Byronic
savagery might have had its hold, but nowadays
nobody is Byronic any more. There is a mysterious force about them, for some mountains are
as sheerly ugly as any slum. Yet I would rather
be there than roaming among pleasures and palaces.
Is it that they are lonely? Is it that they are austere,
defensive, defiant, independent? Of course, that is
the pathetic fallacy (or enslaving modern fashion);
but if one led them to breed those feelings in oneself,
then some of their hold would be accounted for.

Certain I am of one thing, and that is that the
purely æsthetic appeal of the mountains plays but
a very small part in their power. As objects of
beauty they will not hold water for a moment, and
the very frenzy of enthusiasm with which one
worships the Cimon della Pala is the best measure
of one's secret feelings about the obvious short-
comings of the ugly Grigna, or the Grimsel, or
the northern face of the Marmolata, or all such other
spectacles of the Alps as have only the impressiveness of size, which to everyone but a confirmed

megalomaniac is no impressiveness at all.   We are
a flock of sheep, and now that mountains are in
fashion, we pretend an indiscriminate worship.
This is nonsense.   The vast majority of mountains,
like the vast majority of people, are not beautiful
at all, though even many of the worst of them may
have, like Katisha, some hidden charm of shoulder
or heel or flank somewhere lurking round the
corner.

   No, it is in loneliness and lack of motive and the
solemn splendour of their air that the secret charm
of the mountains consists.   I know well that they
are very often rude and angry and ugly ; I puzzle
again and again to analyze what it is I really find
in them.   And my conclusion always is that anyhow
I would (usually, and for my best moments) rather
be alone on the ugliest mountain of the Grimsel or
the Cottians than in the finest palace ever made by
man.   The deepest reason (for pure light and air
and solitude are only contributories) in reality is, I
am sure, that on the mountains one is less than ever
distracted from one's peace.   Their utmost ugliness,
barrenness, grimness, is no enemy to calm, no friend
to the tiresome fusses that on earth intercept one's
clearness of serenity.   In fact, by long roads of
personal inquiry, I come back at last to the know-

ledge of the Lord Buddha (and the great saints before and after) that in the high places of the world the being is better able to look itself undisturbed in the face, and learn the truth and the true proportions of things. And I believe that it is some glimmering knowledge of this that in these latter days has turned the hungry race of western men instinctively towards the mountains, in half-conscious sense of craving for some philosophy of calm, some grip and balance among the worries of life. The sight of a mountain, even from some back-garden in a slum, is a dim reminder that there are other thing than slums, and other gardens than those at the back. And I am certain that the man with such a view from his strip would ultimately prove better and happier than his neighbour who only looks out on a gasworks ; so long, that is, as he sometimes looks at his mountain.

This is very true and helpful, I have no doubt, but my present concern is merely to tell you that the view from the Falzarego is something to go out for to see ; ranging from the central mass of the Marmolata, over the ruffled gleaming snowfields beyond and beyond, and away in the south to where on the edge of the distance the Pala Dolomites stand in a row like a range of soft blue flames. So the

motor slithers down from the pass, through tunnels
and round bends that show an even greater engineering skill than those on the Cortina side of the
pass. On the way you will see to your right,
lonely on a rock, the most fascinating little castle
in the world. It is entirely contained by the square
boulder on which it stands, some fallen relic, in ages
long gone by, of the ragged mountains behind. It
is ruined now, and roofless, but the four walls still
stand, although the built-on portions and the stairs
have fallen away. Behind, it looks up to the range
of the Sasso di Stria, and in front, down over the
deep Livinallongo, towards Marmolata and Civetta.
This is the Castle of Andraz, which I have loved
from first sight, and never pass without longing to
buy it, and restore it, and live in lonely peace among
the hills there, conveniently close to a motoring
highroad.

Down comes the road at last into Pieve di
Livinallongo. Pieve stands high above the valley
whose name it bears, on the slope of a mountain so
steep that the ground-floor rooms of the Hotel
Pieve must be some thirty feet from earth on their
outer side. The Cordevole River runs far below, in
a deep bed almost at right angles to the Falzarego
Pass, flowing down towards Caprile and Civetta

and Pelmo. Look back now from Pieve; the end
of the valley is blocked by the giant tower and twin
buttresses of Pelmo; and Civetta, only less magnificent and overpowering, rises to the right, above
the far-down gleam of the Lago d'Alleghe, lying
in the lap of a mountain-fall just below Caprile.
Glorious enough is the mass of Civetta, rising in
straight ribs to heaven like a pyramid of colossal
organ-pipes; but Pelmo, from wherever you may
see him, is a splendour beyond words and name.
He is not among the first six in point of height,
but there is about him a mysterious might and
majesty. He is more clearly alive than many
another higher mountain; you feel that he is a
thing of enchantment. He is always changing
shape, and always not only splendid, but magical.
From one point he is a vast cathedral of domed
towers; then a demon throne, rounded, dark, and
lowering; then he becomes a wizard castle, austere
and impregnable; and then a sullen, hunched, great
eagle, brooding solemnly over the lesser ranges.

But now the road turns its back upon Civetta
and Pelmo, winding upwards, past little gates and
fortresses—for now we are near the frontier again;
Civetta and Pelmo are in Italy—towards the heights
of the Pordoi. New mountains come into sight at

the head of the valley, the glowing, sheer walls of
the Sella group towering up above the grassy slopes
of Alps that are yet so far above our heads. On our
left, across the stream of the Cordevole, down in
Livinallongo, far beneath us, towers a high jagged
range of blackness, strange among the Dolomites.
For here is an outbreak of igneous rock, bursting up
amid the magnesian limestone of which the district
is built; and on that black ridge, accordingly, there
are marvels to be shown you. That dark wall,
however, cannot yet be popular in our eyes; for
looming overhead it acts as an unwelcome screen to
the glories of the Marmolata, which stands immediately behind, across the gulf of the Fedaja Pass.
Indeed, we shall now be circling the Marmolata all
day, yet hardly, if ever, get another glimpse of her,
except from the heights of the Pordoi.

The road winds up past Arabba, and by the
divergence which goes over the hills to Corvara
and Colfosco. More and more magnificent it
becomes as it mounts towards the pass, climbing
in tight hairpin curls up in the wild Alpine valley
of grass and Rhododendron that leads to the Pordoi.
This drive has a rare beauty; the ascent is austere
and bare between the bare vastness of the mountains; the weird black Sasso di Capello, with its

ragged needles of darkness impending high above you on the left, and in front all the rosy walls and broad domed masses of the Boe and the other huge blocks of the Sella group. In spring the grass is full of flowers, and the height of the pass, limestone though it be, is snowed under with the gentle blooms of the Sulphur Anemone.

And in autumn again, when the air is sad and keen, the pass is no less beautiful, with the bright gold of the dying vegetation, the deep reds of the Alpine evergreens, and the blood-scarlet of the dwarf Buckthorn. Exactly on the summit you will now find, too, accommodation as fine and lavish as anything you could require, in the newly opened Christomannoshaus—no ordinary inn, but the largest and most sumptuous of all the Alpine club-huts, except, perhaps, the one on the Schlern. But in the heights of the season, remember to order your rooms here (and everywhere along the Dolomitenstrasse); and above all, remember that places in the motor have to be booked as far in advance as those for the latest " Dotty Widow," or " Sunshine Sillies." Otherwise whole days may be wasted in delay; though how can one say "waste" of such a sojourn? And yet, even if there is no place, as I believe, in the Dolomites, where one should not be glad to be delayed, still, stoppages, and the disordering of one's plans, are always tiresome, more especially when brought about by some lack of care or forethought in oneself.

I have never yet had time to stay on the Pordoi. And, indeed, until this season there would have been little hope of comfort in so doing; for the old inn was weak in amenities, and the large Hotel Pordoi sits some way down on the slope towards Canazei, a habit that I hate in these pass-hotels, and have already comminated in the case of the Falzarego. A pass-hotel should occupy the very crest of the pass itself, or what is the use of it? We want to make the best of all possible worlds, alike the one in front and the one behind. Now, however, there is no longer any excuse for leaving the Pordoi in a hurry. And there can be no more beautiful place on earth for a stay. In front you have the flamelike wonder of the Langkofel group across the unguessed depths of the valley beneath; on your right the walls and Agia Sophia-like dome of the Boe; and behind you, glowing far away above the edge of the world, all the glowing mountains that you left in attendance upon Cortina.

Endless are the expeditions from the Pordoi

(which it is already obvious that I love far better than the Falzarego), whether you adventure up among the club-huts on the Sella group, quite easy of attainment from here, by paths much easier than those which lead the aspiring along my Cliff-garden at home; or merely wander on the green levels of the Bindelweg, which curls up a pleasant footpath over the shoulder of the rocky little hill above the Christomannoshaus, and then goes almost flat, in and out of the green folds of the hills on the other side, along the sunny slope of the black Padon chain which had loomed over our ascent to the Pordoi; and with a full view the whole way of every foot of the Marmolata, her stupendous glaciers and snowfields, and the buttressing peak of the Great Vernel. This is a perfectly beautiful and easy stroll, and the view momentous. But I have other and much better reasons for directing you along the Bindelweg. For I first knew it from the other approach, by which one climbs in long and tiresome zigzags from the Fedaja Pass down under the Marmolata, until one has reached the upper level, after which the path continues flat to the Pordoi. I was hot and rather cross with the exactions and the floral dulness of the climb by the time I had attained to the dulcet flatness

that one enjoys for the rest of the way. And
then on a heap of stone by the very path-side
I saw some splashes of blue, and suddenly thought I
was going mad. For there was *Eritrichium nanum.*

How light-foot did I run up the slopes and
cliffs of the black Belvedere overhead! And even
from afar those sombre cliffs were tinged with
a faint veil of blue from the turquoise cushions
of Eritrichium with which they are spattered and
strewn. Never was there so riotous a sight of
glory. I had no eyes for *Androsace helvetica*
here miserably occurring, for the first time in
my experience, on volcanic rock ; and swiftly toiled
up to the crest of the ridge, over ever-widening
and more numerous tuffets of silver fluff, mosaicked
with their mass of azure Forget-me-nots. See
it often as you may—and by now I am growing
almost hardened to its temptation—Eritrichium
remains indisputably the king of one's Alpine sens-
ations. Almost hardened, though, say I with
sorrow. For I am growing to believe it a real
crime to disturb Eritrichium from his home, so
obstinately hostile does he almost always remain
to our utmost efforts in the way of hospitality.
The wetness of our climate is something he will
not and cannot be made to endure.

In all these years I have again and again collected Eritrichium, and toiled with him as one
would hardly toil with a sick baby. I have had
many brief delusions of success ; but they all
vanished with the earliest November rains. Never
have I done so well, either, with any subsequent
Eritrichiums as with the very first I ever found,
gleaming in patches of blue jewel-work on the
crest of the Angstbord Pass. Whether that was
some form of special vigour I cannot say ; in any
case, Eritrichium has too often of late years made
me feel a murderer. And yet, and yet, how shall
a gardener resist a temptation keener than any
St. Antony ever underwent, or with idle trowel
tramp ridges and fields of such Eritrichium as you
will see in wide patches of sky all along the rim of
the Belvedere and the Padon Chain ?

I could not resist, nor did I try to. Rarely
have I had happier hours than those I spent in
dalliance with Eritrichium on the edge of the
Belvedere. And I cannot tell you much about the
view, I fear, except that on the one side of you rose
the mass of Marmolata, shimmering white and blue,
while on the other the Ampezzo Dolomites ranged
rosily along the uttermost horizon. And very far
away in the east, beyond Civetta, beyond Pelmo,

beyond Tyrol and Italy, there hung in the palpitating golden haze of the distance a shadowy pale cone, soft as a cloud, and beautiful as a dream, that can have been no less than the Terglou, towering over the Julian Alps and the hills of Carniola. Anyhow, it is hard to find a view that can rival Eritrichium. I scrambled and tight-roped along the ridge in blind and perfect bliss ; for now I am on the very crests to which the road of the Pordoi so respectfully looks up to from far below. A succession of blank precipices falls beneath one's feet, and for the most especially magnificent tufts of Eritrichium you always have to make traverses across the most terrible rock-faces, or skirt the most awe-inspiring gullies. Need I say that in the most impossible place of all there shone a snow-white Eritrichium, with flowers half again as big as usual, and variegated leaves with a golden margin ?

How gingerly and Agag-like I made my way, trying again and again, pulled back by the cowardice of solitude in perilous places, and perpetually called on to one more effort by the gleam of that snowy marvel, the culmination of many years' ambition. Very nasty is that rocky crest of the Padon Chain to play on. It sinks away in a condition of utter collapse, ragged and sheer, to the slopes below ;

straight down between one's heels the Dolomiten-
strasse goes winding and looping like a little white
snake in very bad convulsions.   And the broken
rim of the mountain is a sort of loose conglomerate
of rounded pebbles, which gives way at a touch,
and plunges into the depths with the roar of a
cannonade, in a cloud of sombre dust.   As I had no
wish to make part of that fusillade, or be used as a
projectile upon the innocent fields beneath, I had
to look to my movements with double attention,
prodding every stone before I could trust it, and
never venturing on a hold unless certain of another
to fall back on.   Even so, and after a score of trials,
I could do no better than scramble up and just
poke off some fragments of that clump, in the faint
hope that I might succeed in striking them.   Vain
and stupid delusion !   Where well-rooted plants of
Eritrichium sternly refuse to do anything but die,
what hope is there from mere fragments, that they
will condescend to root and thrive ?   However, I
made hope my comfort in that moment of mutilated
triumph.   After all, it was something to have seen
the albino Eritrichium.   As Adams and Leverrier
knew by the knowledge that is stronger than sight
that there was a further planet yet beyond the
orbit of Uranus, long before the microscopic orb of

Neptune was brought to sight and recognized, even so for years had I known that there must be somewhere, in some blessed ridge or cliff of the world, a snow-white Eritrichium. So was my faith ironically recognized in the end.

All along that Padon Chain, too, there are other treasures of the highest places. Down on the grassy slopes beneath there is *Primula longiflora*, and in turfy places of the crest *Primula minima* is lingering in flower in August ; but on the sheer and terrible face of the broken ridge there are also the typical flowers of the highest non-calcareous rocks— thus to be seen by the ambitious with a very minimum of effort, seeing that you get up to within a few hundred feet of their level on the Pordoi by motor, stroll thence along the flatness of the Bindelweg, and so up to the ridge in half an hour from the path at the very outside. Thus, therefore, have you the easiest chance I know anywhere in the Alps of seeing *Geum reptans* at home, great suns of gold amid the blasted black rock, growing here in unusual situations, on the slithering edges of the cliff, instead of in the rocky hollows and laps in which you generally find it ; and *Ranunculus glacialis* here and there, succulent with its juicy great pink blossoms, sprouting from the cinder-dust between the boulders ; and *Androsace alpina* (*glacialis*), most surprising of all, appearing as a plant of dry crevices and ledges of the cliff instead of forming wide mats in the moist, fine shingle of the highest moraines and shingles.

Indeed, the plant itself is different here : never in the high places of the Dolomites have I found the shingle-haunting Androsace of the Oberland ; it is always a thing of smaller development in these parts, occurring in any number of little tufts, but rarely growing into the big masses that are so glorious in the central ranges. And the flowers in this form are always of the purest white, instead of that entrancing soft rose-pink, rich and gentle, which is such a miracle of beauty in the moraines of the Schwarzhorn and the Dossenhorn and the Stelvio (the only other very high place which I can now think of which takes you up in carriageable comfort to the kingdom of the highest Alpines, where the Glacier Buttercup and *Primula glutinosa* grow by the acre, thick as bluebells in an English wood).

On the other hand, the Dolomite Androsace is perhaps a trifle less impossible in cultivation, and is not quite so grudging of its flowers in our gardens, where the Oberland type gives you only two or

three wizen little pale stars to a wide tuffet, instead
of its normal mats of rosy snow that have tempted
you into bringing it home because it looks so
magnificently free and easy. And you will be
lucky if you get so far as your two or three wizen
stars with *Androsace alpina* from the Oberland ;
the Dolomitic form is at least not wholly disinclined
to survive. And for so much you may be grateful ;
it is a rare quality among the high Alpine Andro-
saces, even rarer than they usually are themselves.

Then one scrambles and toboggans somehow
over the little cliffs and long, steep grass-slopes
down to the path again, thanking one's stars that
the Padon Chain is not so inaccessible on its
southern side as on its northern. Laden with
treasures and memories, we return along the level
Bindelweg to the Christomannoshaus. And here I
will suggest the convenience of these motor-roads.
For, wherever there is such a public service passing
two or three times a day, you can alight at the
hotel, spend as many days as you choose exploring
the delights of its neighbourhood ; and then, when
the fancy takes you, go on by the next motor that
comes by. Even if it should happen to be full, you
can always be glad to wait for the next, or, if time
vehemently press, telegraph beforehand for a place.

Now from the Pordoi the road begins to coil downwards, first over a broad meadow of flowers, greener and softer than that on the northern side, where in autumn the seed heads of the Sulphur Anemone stand wild and ghostly in their silvery towzles, and then through woodland, past the Hotel Pordoi, into the densities of the forest; while overhead to your right the wall of the Boe shoots momentarily higher and higher in the sky. The Sella group is very grand—I will only say that it is a tremendous pedestal with nothing particular on top. From so overwhelming a base of walls, from such a mass, one expects rather more in the way of an apex than is provided by the comparatively insignificant little mounds that crown the bulk of the Boe and the Pordoi-spitze. On the other hand, those walls are crushingly impressive in their mere height and starkness; the time to see them at their grimmest is in some afternoon of brewing thunder, when a violet darkness hides the summits, and throws an ominous revealing gloom upon the walls, intensifying their pinkness to a lurid note, and bringing into prominence the wet-looking stains of black with which they are splashed. As the road comes down, it seems at some points to be driving into an impasse between those sheer faces of rock,

the one rising up overhead into the invisible sky,
and the other facing you in adamantine splendour.
And up above the wind wails mournfully, and
thunder croons among the summits, hidden in that
lowering heaviness of cloud.

But, if the Boe be a plinth without a statue, like
Monte Piano on an immeasurably vaster scale,
then, just opposite, in face of you, all the way
down from the Pordoi, you have a mass of statuary
without a pedestal. Straight up from the grassy
Alps that rise from the woodland so far below, the
Langkofel screams to the sky, a bunch of jagged
flames, like the funeral pyre of some giant arrested
suddenly and immortalized in stone. The Langkofel
out-dolomites the wildest dolomites; it is *super-
echt-Dolomitisch*. There is no group in the whole
district quite so surprising, exaggerated, tormented,
wild. It dominates the whole of the upper Fassa
Valley, crowds out of one's notice the good-natured
elephantine bulk of the Boe, and only goes down
at last in one's memory before the savage and
effortless supremacy of the Cimon della Pala.
Beyond them, as one descends, it is all one can do
to notice the more ample and sterling splendour of
the real Fassa Dolomites farther south, the clustering domes and pyramids round the highest dome of

all, which is King Laurin's Rosengarten. And thus at length the road makes its final close circlings, and comes down into the greenness of the Fassathal, which only a few minutes before had seemed so remote and maplike beneath one's wheels.

CHAPTER VI

AT the head of the Fassathal, immediately at the foot of the Pordoi Pass, there sits a sumptuous hotel where limbs worn flat with the hardnesses of mountain huts may regain their pristine plumpness, and appetites sated with *Rindfleisch* and *Rostbraten* recuperate upon more delicate meats. Otherwise, but for the Dolomitenhaus, I do not know why one should stay at Canazei for long. The place is in a hole, under the Langkofel, under the Boe, and with only the Great Vernel in sight up the lateral valley of the Fedaja Pass. On the other hand, Canazei is a great centre, for thence you may range up among the club-huts of the Boe, the Langkofel, and the Rosengarten groups, while immediately opposite run two charming side valleys, each to a pass under the Marmolata, the one beneath its northern slope, the Fedaja, and the other at the foot of its fearful southern wall, the Contrinjoch.

Each of these has huts and hostelries ; from what I have twice experienced of the Fedaja, and from what I have heard of the Contrin, I judge that this latter is the more delightful of the two.

To reach the Fedaja one continues along up from Canazei, past Penia, up the valley of the Avisio, which comes down from the Fedaja in a succession of waterfalls (rare in these ranges, where running water is a common joy, but cascades of curiously infrequent occurrence on any spectacular scale). Straight in front and overhead looms the naked huge pyramid of the Great Vernel, which, beautiful as it is, yet rouses one's indignation as being all that one can see from Canazei of the Marmolata. The way wanders through a mossy woodland at first, where on the fallen boulders are silvery masses of *Saxifraga squarrosa* and *S. crustata* (which often, but not always, replaces *S. Aizoon* in the lime-stones of the Dolomites ; its leaves are even more beautiful and silvery, its flowers dowdier in the same note of dullish creamy-white). Soon the road climbs steeply, traverses a smooth expanse, and then begins to toil steeply upward again. You have, if my memory serves you, some three steepish pitches on the way up to the Fadaja, of which the last is much the stiffest, but also much

the more interesting, under rocks that are bushy
with Edelweiss (here for once growing as a rock-
plant) and the banks a-wave with the living sapphire
of the Willow Gentian. The Orange Ragwort, neat
and dwarf, with silver leaves, strikes its flaring note
of violent scarlet-gold, as my utmost efforts—and
goodness knows why, for never did a plant look so
willing, nor are Ragworts usually coy—have so far
usually failed to make it do with me. The Baldo
Anemone, too, runs about among the stones, and
in the river-beds shine the lemon-pale globes of the
Rhætian Poppy. The last part of the climb is
under cliffs, past a series of Stations of the Cross
(which, indeed, has long been accompanying you)
and up through woodland, where on the rock-faces
are big masses of *Saxifraga squarrosa*, and pressed
flat rosettes of an Auricula which is light green,
powderless, and quite different from any of the
other forms that I have collected. It is extremely
difficult to extract from the solid rock, and pro-
duces flowers of the most beautiful buttery yellow,
soft, and very pale.

One comes out upon the high lap which is the
Fedaja Pass. Here, on an eminence, is the Bambergerhaus, and a little farther on another inn
for Italians. For here runs the frontier, descend-

ing from the snowfields of the Marmolata, and
running across by the small blue Fedaja Lake,
some half a mile beyond the Bambergerhaus.
Those who have crossed this pass in early summer
fly into quenchless dithyrambs about the glory of
its flowers.   I have twice been there, accordingly,
and thoroughly ransacked its possibilities.   Never
have I found anything of any special interest,
though I must always be grateful to the huge
stone fan that descends from the Marmolata upon
the little lake, for this gave me, many seasons
since, my first unexpected sight of *Potentilla nitida*
in flower.   It was a dull autumnal day, and all the
Marmolata was buried in stone-grey cloud, through
which at intervals the vindictive blue of its glacier
gleamed with the ominous shrillness of glacier ice
in bad weather ; and the flower lay there, glowing
like a little rosy flame among the pitiless white
stones, whence all the other flowers had long since
died away.   I squalled with joy.

But none the less, there was nothing else to see,
nor have I ever found anything else of interest on
the Fedaja ; so that while those fields are no doubt
a perfect blaze of splendour in spring, I think it
must only be in the common way of things
(*Saxifraga Aizoon*, for instance, at last on the

limestone), and though well deserving a visit from the spectacular point of view, is hardly worth the pains of the experienced seeker after floral wonders. It is not, indeed, very wonderful in any other way, either. You see, it is true, the whole of the Marmolata, but you see her from a stone's throw, and from just underneath; beauty and dignity are lost in mere enormousness, seen in too intimate and foreshortened detail to do more than squash you into a stupid acquiescence. You can even be climbing her skirts in a few minutes from the Bambergerhaus, and her presence, shapeless, vast, and white, merely weighs upon you as a wilderness of snowfields, with dumpy domes of rock protruding at intervals to bear up the mass. Nor is the other slope of the valley more inspiring, for straight up behind the Bambergerhaus go steeply climbing the long dull grassy slopes that lead us on to the Bindelweg under the Padon Chain above. Even the distant view over into Italy is restricted and blocked by uninteresting masses near at hand, though in the distance when Civetta glows like a furnace at sunset, there is, indeed, something to sit among the pines and dream of afterwards.

Many travellers come over the Fedaja from Caprile. My experience has always been in the reverse direction, and it was in tragedy that my acquaintance with the Fedaja began. I had lured my companions up there on a day that clearly threatened rain, and it was our scheme to strike away over the range to our left from the pass, under Padon, and so rejoin our carriage at Pieve di Livinallongo, for the passing of the Falzarego on the morrow. It was a threatening day, as I tell you ; but long experience has taught me that you can nearly always bluff the clerk of the weather. With awful signs he tries to daunt you, but if you go on boldly, never minding, and refusing even to consider the possibility of disaster, then generally the clouds will scatter, and the sun come out, and the day prove glorious. Thus it has happened to me times beyond number, and I still think it would so have happened on this occasion also had it not been that my cousin was wearing a clean pair of white flannels. Providence can stand a good deal in the way of temptation, and the clerk of the weather is respectful to a bluff of decent boldness ; but this was too much effrontery for the one, and too violent a temptation for the other. It was the last straw that broke their endurance.

We started ; all the hills were stony cold, and

above their summits lay banks of ragged gloomy cloud that drew momentarily lower. By the time we reached the Bambergerhaus, the Marmolata had retreated wholly into primal darkness, from which only at intervals would balefully glare the green luminosity of some crevasse far up in the snowfields among the drifting seas of greyness. No rain as yet, but the air grew rapidly colder and more ominous. Also, I had found no plants of the slightest interest, and even if I had, the joy would only have been bitterness. For the beloved trowel of many seasons had, after many thrilling escapades upon the mountains, been tamely lost at last in Bozen, and my utmost searches in that city had only succeeded in providing me with a common garden-trowel of the usual ample curve. And to any of you who have an enemy, I would only urge that you set him to dig Alpine plants in stony ground with an ordinary garden-trowel. You will never dislike him again after that : he will have paid off all his debt in full. However, our disasters were still but brewing.

At the Bambergerhaus we lunched, and lounged a little by the lake, and then prepared to fare forward on our way. And at once we went wrong. Of course, as I now know, we should have struck sharp away to the left, at right angles, up under Padon, along the path that leads across the range to Pieve ; instead, seeing no such path, we continued directly downwards, not realizing that we were thus making straight for Caprile. Down we went, and down and down and down. On our right rose the huge white walls of the Marmolata, and on the other the mountain-ranges grew higher and higher at every step. We knew we had to cross them somewhere, and every step made it plain that worse and longer would ulti-mately prove the ascent we should have to make towards our pass over to Pieve. My cousin and I looked at each other with blank eyes of perplexity. We had an aunt with us that day (*the* Aunt, let me say), whom we were chivalrously afraid of fatiguing. Quite needlessly, in point of fact, for that same aunt is amply capable of wearying out a team of mules on the mountains, and then being fresh for billiards and piquet all night. None the less, after a long day we dreaded for the poor lady the grow-ing altitudes of that ridge which we should some-time have to cross, as we still faithfully believed, though gradually suspicion was coming upon us that somewhere we must have strayed from our proper track. At last we met an aged crone, with

a load of hay on her head, and asked her to produce the path to Pieve. For all reply she dropped
her knitting to the ground, raised both her hands
to heaven, and began keening shrilly, like one
bereft of hope. Through her dismal wails we
ultimately succeeded in gathering the extent of
our disaster: we had wholly missed the way from
the top of the Fedaja! Between us and Pieve now
towered an impassable wall of mountains. Nothing
remained for us but to continue onwards and onwards with the hypothetically wearied aunt, until at
the end we could lay her exhausted bones at Caprile.

We all looked blue at this news, but the aunt
bore up, and we sternly set to trudging down and
down and down once more in the direction of
Caprile, while overhead the sky darkened more and
more, and the chill wind of autumn blew with an
ominous shrillness across the uplands of withered
seed vessels. Down into the forest zone we got,
and after that plunged into the gorge of the Serraj
de Sottoguda. I have seen many of the big Alpine
cañons, the Gorge de Trient, the Aarenschlucht,
the Gorner ; never have I seen anything more sur-
prisingly impressive than the Serraj de Sottoguda.
It is a ravine deep down between walls of limestone some hundreds of feet high, and so close

together that daylight only filters dimly through the slit above you, and the path has often to be carried out on wooden galleries above the roaring stream. The walls on either hand are dewy with moisture and hung with curtains of moss, and densely set with big silvery masses of *Saxifraga squarrosa*. The whole ravine is about a mile in length, and I never traverse Trow Ghyll, the deep cañon opening up towards the fells of Ingleborough, without being recalled to my memories of the Serraj de Sottoguda.

While we trudged down that close defile the thunder broke. Overhead in the angry sky it shattered and roared, and from the walls of the ravine it rolled and drummed and blattered round and round us. Cracking dry bursts and long blaring carronades re-echoed from the heavens and earth. And then the heavens were loosened, and through the trumpets of the thunder descended the silver lances of the rain. We might crouch and lurk and wait as we pleased ; in ten minutes we were wet to the bone. Finally, after some moments wasted in a dripping cave, we decided to bear up against the worst (seeing that we could be no wetter than we were) and hurry on to the first possible albergo, and there stomach the lack of clothes and luggage, and go to bed immediately between the blankets. We hurried feverishly onwards down the glen, panting for the moment of arrival, when suddenly cries arose in our midst. One of our party had left his German grammar behind ; he had made this useful volume more useful still by using it as a little island of dryness to sit on in that sloughy grotto ; and now, in the hurry of the moment, it had been forgotten. And it had belonged to great-Aunt Fanny, and was therefore precious beyond price ! What was to be done ? Consternation seized us until my cousin, always altruistic, went back up the gorge at a run, leaving us clustered in the rain like a knot of helpless sheep, without even the protection of wool. After what seemed a soaking hour he returned. Certainly the high gods had had their will of those presumptuous white flannels, so neat and clean and nice. The grammar, however, was safe ; he had discovered it in the hands of a peasant woman, who was poring reverently over its mysteries. Heartened by this success we resumed our way, and as soon as we had emerged from the gorge the rain began to mitigate its transports. A little farther, the fallen Republic of Rocca Pietore—the smallest in the world—blessed our eyes upon its little slope in

the valley.   We made eagerly for the Hotel Posta,
and were soon at peace.

I am not going to waste your patience with
recommendations to go and stay at the Hotel
Posta in Rocca Pietore.   But we were completely
happy in that very simple little pot-house.   The
merriment of complete disaster swept over us like
a flood ; without a rag of change, cut off from all
our belongings, we laughed and laughed and laughed
until the walls re-echoed like those of Sottoguda
to the thunder.   And our good hosts laughed also,
and were cordial and sympathetic and hilarious as
only Italians have the gift of being in some lone
albergo among the hills or vine-clad valleys.   I
remember what amusement we afforded—we and
our wants and our wetness and our Italian—to the
presiding Hebe of the inn, a charming maiden
named Tita, marred only, like Miss Letitia Hawky,
with a " trifling obliquity of vision."   And meanwhile the thunder had again descended with the
night, and the blue darkness of the hills was
shattered every second by white and blinding
blasts of light that hardly attempted to keep time
with the crashing furies of the thunder that en-
veloped us all round, while the rain roared down
on the roof like a river.   We discarded any notion

of sending on my cousin through the storm to tell the coachman, patiently waiting at far-off Pieve, what it was that had happened to delay his fares. We supped riotously instead upon *Risotto* from a common bowl, and retired to our beds. And in the morning, behold a day as crystal-clear, glorious, and blue as only a day in the hills after violent thunder can ever be.

So we made our farewells to Tita, and pursued our way towards Caprile, whose look did not draw my fancy, though its situation is singularly happy, close to the little green Lago d'Alleghe (created a century and more ago by a landslide from the Monte Forca), and immediately at the foot of Civetta's huge façade of soaring organ-pipes. Then we turned away up a track to our left, opposite the stone-tumble of the Sasso da Ronch across the valley, like a number of towers fallen higgledy-piggledy, and so along over the shoulders of the hill, in and out of its wide bays, across the frontier where a charming *douanier* had a long domestic chat with us, and ultimately, after a final curl in and out that almost broke our hearts, up to Pieve, that had looked so close above us, until we found that we had to sweep right into the heart of the range and round again.

And every time I have since passed through
Pieve I have wondered whether our losing our way
that day was not after all a blessing in (singularly
complete) disguise.   For I have often subsequently
marked the way we ought to have taken, down
from the towering crest of Padon ; it is long and
far, but, above all, at the end, when we should have
been weary, all of us, the path has to take a fearful
plunge right down into the gulf of the Livinallongo,
and then climb up and up and up again interminably
to Pieve, just opposite, a couple of stone-throws
across the valley.   Even the most cast-iron of
aunts might well have been exhausted by such
a jaunt, made all in the one day from Canazei.
As it was, we made a gentle day and a half
of it.

To Canazei I now return.   The only way to do
this is over the Pordoi, an opportunity I gladly
take of retraversing ground so beautiful and beloved.   In Canazei we rest once more a little and
grow fat ; then continue in the motor down the
Fassathal.   The Fassa Valley is deep and green
and beautiful ; at intervals on either hand rises the
thorny hedge of Dolomites.   But they are usually
too close overhead to be seen above the lower
woods, except where great flames of soaring rock

loom in the sunset above Campitello or Vigo.   As
you look back at the head of the valley, the mass
of the Boe, sumptuous and solemn, blocks the
view; and to the left rise up the screaming pinnacles
of the Langkofel.   And though the Fassathal is
a little low for those who want to be easily up in
the heart of the hills, it is very peaceful and
delightful in itself, broad and fertile between its
enclosing ranges, and watered with a stream
more brilliant than blue jewels.   In autumn
all the fields are thick-set with the amaranth
of Autumn Crocus.   In a field by Vigo I saw
two white ones as I was whirled helpless by
one day.

One year I paused in the lower Fassathal.   It
was my ambition to go up the Monzonithal,
which is a divergence from the Val San Nicolo,
opening out opposite a little place called Pozza.
There, accordingly, I thought I would stay.   I
alighted therefore at the Leone d'Oro.   And it was
too dreadful.   They had evidently never had any
staying guest there before ; the very idea almost
drove them to tears.   And the only room they
offered was manifestly impossible.   There was
nothing for it but to retreat bag and baggage up
the road, some half-mile or more to Perra.   And

here, exhausted by the hot sun and the dusty road, we tumbled into the first hotel we came to: a shuttered place, but of cleanly and comfortable pretensions, far more alluring to my taste than the starred Hotel Rizzi just beyond, by a huge boulder fallen from the mountain, which in shape or proportion reminds me of something seen in China or Japan.

In point of fact, here one is in a mixed land, neither Austrian nor Italian, but Ladin, whatever that may be, though the august name still clearly emerges from beneath this disguise. But these Latins have a strange jargon of their own, and are a race apart in these lone valleys, some backwash from the time when the Empire was breaking, and the nations in fusion. Never elsewhere in the wildest Alps of Italy have I had any such rebuff to my feelings as I met with in the Leone d'Oro at Pozza. Never have I met with anything but the most perfect cleanliness and charm of life, even in places the most remote, where the simplicity of ways and food was most complete. I say this with confidence and joy, but I say it only as a man. Women, we know, have a miraculous insight into dust and dirt where happier man sees only a pleasant swept and garnished tidiness. Women, in fact, as the One Jane has quoted from the inmost heart of man, " will always have their little nonsenses and needless cares."

So I come back to the Hotel Piaz in Perra, with words of recommendation on my lips, and self-congratulation that Fate was kind enough to waft me there. My welcome and entertainment were all that I could ask. The house belongs to one of the most illustrious of the Dolomite guides ; the dining-room is frescoed round with his most sensational first-ascents. It was there that I made my earliest acquaintance with Edmondo's Julia, looking as hairy as any Struwwelpeter ; and then, never knowing where she was, lifted lazy eyes one day long after from the lawn at Misurina, with difficulty discerned an obelisk standing out from the wall of the Popena ridge, and gave a cry of recognition—" There, there is the Julia of Edmondo de Amicis !"

In point of fact, I will now go back on my own words, or yield for a moment to human selfishness. Beautiful as is the Fassathal, there are really too many people in it either for my comfort or their own. Go there in June : all is well, and you have it to yourself; but between the 10th and 14th of July the whole picture changes at a few hours' notice, with the break-up of mercantile and educational establishments throughout Germany and Austria. Whereas the day before you had the motors and hotels to yourself, and "wandered lonely as a cloud" through the corridors, and had big pink trout all to yourself, now suddenly every diligence is groaning and bulging with its burden. You have to order your rooms beforehand in the hotels, your fish becomes a ragged fag-end devoured in a roaring horde, and even the motors, so much more expensive than the poor old hot horse-diligences that still toil painfully and heavy-laden over the passes, are now so crowded that forethought and diplomacy are necessary if you are to get your seat in time.

Nor are the irrupters of a nature to cajole your love ; they are an unalluring and stuffy tribe, these male and female trampers—at least to the prejudiced Britisher, clad in the very irreducible minimum of necessary clothing, who opens astonished eyes upon the vast female bunches that may be met on the high passes, and on their menkind, scarlet and perspiring, in layers of the heaviest velveteen or frieze over the thickest possible of Jaeger underclothing, painfully visible between the loose breeches and the ungartered (always ungartered) stockings

into which its grey bulges are tucked. And this
is a sample of the conversation that rages in the
motors of the lovely Fassathal in August: " Und
dann haben wir Hu-u-uhn-mayonnaise gegessen."
This with a glutinous roll that baffles the re-
sources of the typewriter. Swift comes the
answer: " Aber, dass war herr-r-rlich !" with an
equal deep glutinousness of appreciation. And so
on, and so on, with cluckings and sighings of
appreciation throughout a lengthy *menu*, while all
the time the Langkofel and the Boe are flying by.
Fortunately, at this moment our car, a very old
one (in use only that day as a relief service), from
having been crawling uphill with unexampled
slowness, suddenly began to limp and groan and
stagger in the most alarming manner. It then
emitted a mass of dun-coloured smoke, and immediately burst into a sheet of flame. Instantly,
by some process that I have never fathomed, the
whole load of us, even the oldest and the stoutest,
were out in the road, without apparently the movement of a muscle. The banks were littered with
Baedekers and cloaks, and we were all frenziedly
hurling earth from the ditches upon the conflagra-
tion. Ultimately we got it out, and then had to
retreat downhill to a neighbouring village, where,

alas! there was no hope of *Huhn-mayonnaise,* to wait while another car was being sent up from Predazzo.   My last memory of that motor is of an astonished little ant crawling perplexedly about on the sparking-plug, to which she had innocently been transplanted in some clod of earth.

CHAPTER VII

INTO the Monzonithal I mean to take you, if only for a sight of the flowers that there prevail. You go up in the valley of San Nicolo, opposite Perra or Pozza, through delicious pinewoods, till you come to a small chapel where the track diverges to the right and mounts towards the Monzonithal, at first through forest still, and then over meadows, and then across a tumble of stones, which brings you ere long to the Taramelli Hut, sitting on a little hummock by itself, just at the foot of the final ascent into the Monzonithal. The Taramelli Hut, however, is one of those rare refuges where you can only get food, and not, I believe, a bed ; it is merely a small box perched upon a lump of rock.

Now one abruptly mounts the slope of the mountain towards the crags of rose and red and grey that are so alluring on the sky-line from Pozza ; for this lower part of the Fassathal and its

southern extremity (which is called the Fleimserthal) forsake the primitive purity of dolomite, and
erupt into every kind of volcanic and igneous
fantasy in the way of porphyry and syenite. With
the result that here you have a true dolomitic mass
of rosy grey, and next door a sombre peak of purple
or brown; with the further, and to me more
valuable, result also that here you get the dolomitic flora in full splendour, and then again, next
door, and no less lavish, the high Alpines of granitic
persuasion, flourishing not a yard beyond their
calcareous friends, where the formation changes
suddenly. For first proof of this, as soon as you
have mounted that first slope, on which the open
patches are glorious with the violet and gold of
Linaria alpina in great masses (for this is a plant
which often seems anti-calcareous), you come out
upon a long slope of coarse red igneous blocks,
across which the path goes level towards a little
neck beyond. And here at once there are thick
jungles of the Glacier Buttercup, glowing rosy
among the redness of the rocks. (It always seems
to me much rosier on the fire-born formations than
on sandstones such as the Schwarzhorn moraine
where it only goes pink later in its day, but makes
a general effect of white, round flowers at its climax.

This may, however, only be—though I do not
think so—that in the Oberland and Engadine I
have struck it usually at an earlier point of the
summer.) Not only, too, are there jungles of the
Glacier Buttercup, but waving coppices of *Geum
reptans*, rooting far and wide through the chaos,
and covered with its big golden suns, or the silvery
fluff-whirls of its seed.

I was out that day for the hybrid Primulas
between *minima* and *glutinosa*, and as August was
well in, my heart was wrung with anxiety as to
whether I should find them still in flower even at
such a height as the Monzonithal. It is very
possible for the practised eye to spot the hybrids by
their leaf alone, but it means poring over the
ground closely with back bent and bowed like some
aged crone. I have often done it, but the added
labour is so great that one is overjoyed to be helped
by the glow of a flower. Therefore it was with a
sigh of joy that just beyond the red stone-slope on
the little neck, I came suddenly upon my first
flower-heads of the Sticky Primrose, richly violet
among the grass, while higher up the bank there
lurked a few lingering carbuncles of the Fairy
Primrose. Yes, I know well how horribly inadequate it is to use jewel-similes for flowers or

skies ; one exhausts a whole jeweller's shop on a
sunset, and not one of the precious stones thus
roped in has really anything to do with the case.
No sky or mountain anywhere was ever like
sapphires or topaz or opal ; the soft living wonder
of the glowing air has no resemblance whatever
to the hard and crystalline brilliance of a dead
stone.   It is only a literary realism that one satisfies
in finding jewel-comparisons for the skies: a
universal tradition which we should now all of us
be unhappy without, and our minor poets in despair.
It would even seem wrong and unsatisfactory
to our tastes to-day if the vault of heaven were not
compared to a sapphire, and a dawn described as
opal, so thoroughly are we drilled by now into the
crying bad taste of the Apokalyptic New Jerusalem,
that jeweller's nightmare.

But if it be absurd to talk thus of the air, how
even more monstrous to speak of the flowers in
terms of crystal ! Sapphire Gentians, indeed,
and ruby Primulas ! Was ever any convention so
grotesque as this, that compares evanescences so
soft and palpitating, with permanent planes and
surfaces and colours so arid and unyielding in their
splendours ? But, alas, there is no other measure
for our delight in the flowers ; and it is possible,

too, that our inmost snobbishness derives a little pleasure from matching them so expensively. What other language is one to use, too ? To go on saying red and rose and pink and purple is to go on saying nothing, to paint no picture in the mind. For no two reds or pinks are the same ; one would want a page of annotations on each if the description is to be fair ; and in the long multiplicity of detail all life and conviction would vanish. Jewels at least have the advantage of calling up a vivid image in the mind, revivifying in a way the flame and sparkle of a flower in sunlight. Even if that image be inadequate and unfair, it at least stamps the word-portrait of a flower with some vitality, and is not weak. Woven fabrics, however, are of course the only possible comparison for the exquisite textures, the sheen and shimmer of a petal. But who is going to dare talk about the pink poplin of a Primula, the satinette of a Godetia, the puce alpaca of some Zinnias, the half-mourning crêpe de Chine of an Oncocyclos Iris, or the inferior grey flannelette of Edelweiss ? Romance perishes at the thought, and even " the sapphire silk of the Gentian," which strikes me suddenly as really rather good, owes its salvation only to the strong note brought in by that inevitable jewel-word.

I have strayed from the little neck beyond the
red stone-bank.   Above it on the right rise long
sweeping slopes to dark igneous mountain.   But
on the left, where the path takes us curving across
the left-hand declivity, the going is over limestone
white as milk.   Here, accordingly, the Sticky
Primrose abruptly ceases, because she abominates
lime ; and the Fairy Primrose ceases also, because
she has no fancy for stone.   Instead, you have the
limestone flora—pale Poppies, the silver Potentilla,
Lilac Thlaspi, Edelweiss, and, in place of *Ranunculus glacialis*, *R. Seguieri*.   Down below to your
right, in a hollow, lies a small green lake ; the
path curves round above this at length, and over
rocky wastes to certain silty earth-ridges that my
eye had marked from far below as being the likely
haunt of *R. parnassifolius*, which had been
reported to me from the Monzoni.   And here
accordingly it was, in abundance in the fine shingle.
But I greatly suspect it ; true to say that it was
not yet in full blossom.   But hunt as I might, I
could nowhere find any flower or sign of flower
that had the proper complement of petals ; they
each had one or two, and the rest of the bloom was
made up of colourless little chaffy tabs.   By so
much they were better, indeed, than *parnassifolius*

from the Piz Padella, which consists wholly of
chaffy tabs and nothing else ; but how far removed
from the full snowy orbs that lie about on the
white mud of the Forcella Lungieres. Accordingly
I continued my way, which now leads on to an
undulating stretch of moor, the culminating cul-
de-sac of the valley, with the pass itself not very far
away ahead, a shallow notch between the long
ragged igneous ranges on the right, and the high
limestone masses overhead on your left. And the
view must be left for you to discover ; I became
much too busy to have any eyes for it.

For suddenly one is upon the igneous substratum
again, with the result that all that moor is spread
with a veil of violet by the incalculable multitudes
of *Primula glutinosa,* sprouting in rich heads of
purple from its neat little tuffets over every ridge
and bank and level of the turf. People are always
apparently making mistakes about this plant—very
unnecessarily, because it is the most easily known
of all, being the only one of our Alpine Primulas
with flowers of a pure violet-blue. You may
imagine how bewilderingly beautiful ; wherever it
does grow it grows by the million, and the granitic
Alps in the southern ranges are carpeted with it at
great elevations. Many of its hills it shares with

Primula minima, which here on the Monzonithal especially, but in many other mountains also, gives rise to a whole series of hybrids, unduly named and classified, which range from huge flowered, twy-flowered *minimas*, close and dwarf as *minima* herself, to bigger flowered, hotter purple *glutinosas*, and then on into *P. Floerkeana*, which has *minima's* wide blossoms, on *glutinosa's* three-inch stem, and glowing with a fiery ruby-lilac wholly of its own, but nearer to the tone of *minima* than to the pure bishop's purple of *glutinosa*. And, while *minima* is easy to grow in fair conditions of care, and *glutinosa* usually difficult under any and every condition, the hybrids are more generally vigorous and robust than either of their parents. But as I do not wish to " impeage " the character of *glutinosa* too severely, I will say that perhaps she is not so much difficult as tricky. She wants cool, peaty soil, moist and well drained ; she will grow with a fair readiness, and if she be shy-flowering at home, well, that she is on her own native hills ; only there she dwells in such dense abundance that though only one clump in five may have sent up flower-heads, the general effect is of a film of violets lying over the moorland.

All the hybrids were there that day in glory,

gleaming from afar with a wholly different note
from either of their parents. Their begetting is
easy. *P. minima* is hardly earlier in flower than
glutinosa, though when *glutinosa* is at its height,
minima can only be found lingering on shady
northern banks. However, of course they have a
long period earlier in the year, during which they
overlap, for the Sticky Primrose seems to have a
more extended period of blossom than many other
Alpines, blooming steadily on from the melting of
the snow until the snows are getting ready to
descend again. A puzzle to me is why the various
forms of the hybrids should be so local. On the
Monzonithal you find a very wide series, in con-
siderable frequency ; but I could see no sign of that
hot purple *glutinosa*-child which is called *P. Salis-
burgensis*. Whereas on the Kraxenträger and the
range of Colbricon I could succeed in discovering
no other. And yet one would have thought that
everywhere the two parents ought to produce the
same set of offspring. One does not expect the
same Mr. and Mrs. Brown to have white children
in London, and black children in Glasgow, and
yellow children in Birmingham, and mulattoes at
Stow-on-the-Wold.

I do not think that the most arrant non-gardener

can grudge me my joy on the upper Monzonithal, nor fail to share it, indeed—all those, at least, who find more beauty and profit in a mass of lovely colour (even if they neither know, nor want to, the names of its constituent elements) than in some hotel frontage or colourless highroad. Therefore will I linger on, and ask my followers to share my rapture in discovering a pure and perfect albino of *Primula glutinosa*. Not, indeed, that any albino is ever so beautiful as the type from which it sports ; only there is the sense of achievement in finding it, and the eager previous day-dreams of how wonderful it must surely be when found, even though one well knows that it will almost certainly turn out to be more frail and feeble in habit and shape than its type. So it was with my white *glutinosa*, which has long since gone the way of all flesh, and many plants ; so it is with the white *minimas*, the white *spectabilis.* So it will be with the white *Wulfeniana*, the white *Clusiana*, the white *glaucescens* when at last I have achieved them.

This expedition to the Monzonithal, though, was indeed my day for albinos, for when at last I tore myself away from their Imperial Stickinesses, and shinned up the black shingle to the ridge on the right of the pass, I found the whole *arête* a

blue blaze of Eritrichium ; and as I worked along
the crest of the pass, I came at last upon another
white one to make up for my disappointment on
the Padon. Alas, it had no better luck, nor longer
life. And then, for the third delusive good fortune,
my brother, who had gone off up the limestone
mass on the left of the pass for the view you get
thence of the southern wall of the Marmolata,
returned with news of having there seen a white
Linaria alpina ; and on my uttering wails of
anguish at his not having got it (he had noticed
me refusing Linarias on the way up as a common
thing, unprofitable to collect roots of, seeing how
it comes from seed ; and this, indeed, it is, but its
albinos are so rare as to be among the *cordons
bleus* of the collector) was saint enough to toil up
that peak again, and fetch it me down. But collected roots of *Linaria alpina* are bad to deal with ;
the plant, though not an annual, has the miffy-
rootedness of an annual, and rarely survives the
stress of being brought home.

Meanwhile, upon the very pass I laboured and
wrought blindly, like the man with the muck-rake,
amid all the miracles of the mountain world.
Below me, down on the other side, the track went
winding gently over grassy meadows to San Pelle-

grino ; and beyond rose the austere ranges towards
the Pala group ; while to the left, behind the rude
and rugged mass of Costabella, shot up the for-
bidding magnificence of the Punta del Uomo.
However, Thlaspi was thick in the limestone
shingle of the pass itself, where the igneous rock
abruptly ceases ; and down the slope in thick white
clayey silt, *Ranunculus Seguieri* was brilliant with
its snowy blooms and fine foliage. Most striking
it was to see, too, how only on that calcareous strip
would it occur ; close at hand the fire-rock began
again, and there at once shot up the rosy masses
of *R. glacialis*. Neither trespassed by one inch
on the territory of the other ; the line of de-
marcation was hard and definite ; nor, though
they grew almost touching, was there any sign of
intermediate offspring, though I suspect *Seguieri*
to be very close to *glacialis* in its original nature.
Postulate a long-vanished archetype, dividing subsequently into two branches, one growing into the
habit of limestone, the other into that of granite,
by force of occurrence, and you have a rough
sketch of what may be the relationship of those
two buttercups.

And in and among *R. Seguieri* rose here
and there the stem of the universal *Anemone*

baldensis. It was with a full heart and a full tin that I returned at last down the Monzonithal. And if the full tin scandalizes the innocent, let me remind them, for the twentieth time at least, that rare plants in the Alps are not rare in quantity, but rare in distribution. Often, indeed, the word "rare" merely means rare in cultivation; for where an Alpine plant is found at all, it is found in such countless millions that to take a hundred specimens away is like taking a saltspoonful out of the sea. I do not think I have ever met with a rare plant whose rarity consisted in paucity of specimens, unless it be, indeed, here and there some special forms of the hybrid Primulas — never the true species. And these, of course, are sacrosanct.

Returning again to Perra we take the motor once more and career down the Fleimserthal, with sheer soaring pinnacles flying past us overhead on either side, through Vigo, where the other motor-road diverges up over to Bozen by the Karer Pass between the masses of the Latemar and the Rosegarden; through Moëna (whence the lovely Lusia Pass takes you over the left-hand ranges to Paneveggio), along the side of the roaring beryl-blue river, now flowing broadly, and now through tall piered gates of purple porphyry, and thus at length to Predazzo, at the junction where the Paneveggio highroad starts up to the left for the Rolle Pass and San Martino de Castrozza.

We change motors at Predazzo for the Rolle Pass. The big hotel at Predazzo where the motors stop is large and good, but for Predazzo as a whole I have a warm dislike. It is hot and stuffy, and dull and dusty. One comes to it only because one must, and I have lingered there simply for the sake of sending off my plants. It is, however, a geologist's paradise, for the geological confusion of the mountains hereabouts becomes perfectly indecent. Everything is upside down and where it should not be. The learned come far to see limestone underlying igneous rock, and other frivolous fantasies of the red-hot ages. As for me, I get as soon as I can into the motor. Do I not see, over the intervening pine-forest, the jagged peaks of the Pala Dolomites, the one redeeming promise of Predazzo? And shall anything keep me for an instant more than necessary from the Rolle Pass and the Cimon della Pala? No!

CHAPTER VIII

EVEN the drive up to the Rolle is beautiful—quite
the most beautiful I know in the Dolomites. At
first you mount over grassy meadows, over which
Salvia pratensis in June spreads one solid sheet of
pure deep purple; and then through a sparse belt
of wood, and then over rolling grassy Alps all set
with the flowers of the upper meadows. The great
Anemones are there, and the spires of St. Bruno's
Lily standing rare and pure in the hollows of the
hayfields. Then you wind among deep woods, high
up on the edge of a gorge, and past a fort, and up
again, until you come to the hotel of Paneveggio.
The hotel is all there is of Paneveggio : it is a large,
comfortable, crowded place, long and low, in which
you will be very wise to book your rooms well
beforehand, after the 10th of July ; for not only is it
in itself a famous centre for *Sommerfrischlers*, who
come *en pension* for the month, but it is also on

the highroad over the Rolle to San Martino de Castrozza, almost as popular a summer-place as Seis, so that its moving population, going or coming, has a great way of stopping a day or two at Paneveggio *en route.*

The hotel lies at the edge of the pine-forest, with ample meadows rolling away on either side. I cannot conceive of a more delightful place for a stay, though I myself never manage to linger long when the high places are close at hand and calling me so loudly. However, if you stay at Paneveggio, you always have the passing motor to take you up to the Rolle at your pleasure, and a returning one to bring you down again, and meanwhile the woods and meadows all about are full of the most delightful leisurely walks, and you may even come on the Cypripedium, in fine fat form, lurking among the copses—a crowning glory that has never yet fallen to my lot in all my years among the hills. One could be very pleasantly and profitably idle at Paneveggio, with the gaunt granitic dome of Colbricon towering high across the valley, and behind you, over the pinewood, the limestone mass of Castellazzo. But the very reason why so many people will enjoy a stay here is also the reason why I myself can never make one. For close overhead,

from every window and balcony of the hotel, you
see just the points of the Cima Vezzana and the
Cimon della Pala peering over the huge bank of
forest on your left.   And at the sight of them, the
itch of high places gets into my blood, and I fidget
over my good dinner, and cannot sit quiet until
I am in the motor that takes me up into their
immediate presence.

The spruce-forest of the Rolle Pass is the finest
I have ever seen in the Alps, unless it be that on the
Rosenlaui side of the Great Scheidegg.   But there
the huge old trees are twisted and gnarled ; on the
final ascent of the Rolle the vast trunks rise solemn
and stately as the pillars in some infinite green
cathedral.   The road winds upward in smooth rapid
curves, and the view widens behind you, and on
your right unfolds the long and jagged igneous
range that so boldly fronts the sovereignty of the
Pala group.   I remember, too, how glorious were
the patches of Spring Gentian in June by the road-
way, almost more splendid than the wide patterns
and single sparks of sky that one sees as one
descends the Pordoi upon Canazei.   At last, however, we are above the forest, traversing a very dull
green Alp, which is the Malga Rolle.   And on our
left towers the tumbled masonry of Castellazzo,

and on our right, Colbricon. And then, straight
in front, breaks suddenly upon us the whole force
of the Cimon della Pala, seen here as one awful
minaret of rock—the culmination and end of the
long sheer scarp of wall that is the view of it
from St. Martino de Castrozza.

But from here the Cimon della Pala is the mountain of mountains. There is nothing like it for the
cruel and naked insolence of its splendour. It is
to me more tremendous than the Viso or the
Matterhorn ; more lonely, more alive in the ever-
lasting defiance of its attitude ; for it is vital limestone, not dead and rotten granite. It is the
super-Dolomite. Marmolata is a queen among
mountains in general, Pelmo is a castle of enchantment, the Drei Zinnen the very perfection of
dolomitic form, the Langkofel its keenest exaggera-
tion ; but the Cimon is a thing to itself, the quint-
essential wonder of them all ; it goes to heaven in
a soaring rush of supremacy—swift, arrogant, merci-
less, and serene. Years since I first saw one of
Mr. Compton's portraits of it : the thing came upon
me as a shock ; I had no notion where such a mountain could be found on earth. But I decided then
and there that I would lay what soul I had at the
feet of the Cimon della Pala. And so I have laid

it ever since. There is no compassing in words or colour the glory of this peak ; but the road now winds down a little dip, and the motor makes its halt at the inn of the Rolle Pass, immediately in front of the Cimon's whole unbearable magnificence. So there one can sit for long hours in the glazed Laube, looking out at that vast needle soaring up across the little intervening valley, and studying all its moods, and the infinite variety of its colouring.

I do not know when the Cimon is most wonderful : whether at dawn, or at midday with torn clouds hovering around it and behind, or lifting it far above the little earthly ranges below ; or yet again at sunset, when the great wall goes red as blood, and strange coils of cloud come twining round it like ghostly dragons from below. So I have watched it flush at sundown from shade to shade of salmon, rose, and apricot to an incandescent scarlet ; soft cloud-banks came up from San Martino, grey and flocculent, in white bosses and undulations, to play peep-bo among the crags of the Sass Maor behind the Cimon, but on the awful peak itself were unable and unanxious to effect any lodgment. At one moment, from some hot, deep embrasure half-way up, the melting snow sent

curling an altar-smoke of brief and evanescent
vapour; but that was all. So the fires culminated
at last, and faded rapidly, leaving the clouds worsted,
and the peaks all standing hard and silent, high
against a vault of violet, that ultimately faded to
a cold and sombre blue.

The Cimon della Pala is not the highest of its
group. And behind it, above San Martino, stand
the Sass Maor, the Pala de San Martino, the
Cima di Ball—the most bewildering assemblage
of splinters and towers standing discreetly in
attendance on the Cimon; to its left is the
respectable mass of the Cima Vezzana, which, in
point of fact, is higher than the 10,450 feet of the
Cimon. This latter, however, almost takes rank as
the sixth among the Dolomites, and used in old
days to be actually ranked as second, thanks to its
own tremendous and easy assertion. At their head
stands the regal Marmolata, with 10,855 feet;
Antelao follows close with 10,710 feet; the third
is Sorapiss, of 10,595 feet, pressed hard by the
10,565 feet of Civetta and Tofana. And then slip
in by a few feet, that one feels to be unfair, the
Cima Vezzana and Cristallo; and only after these the
Cimon della Pala: leaving Pelmo, Boe, Langkofel,
Croda Rossa, Rosengarten, and Drei Zinnen

huddling in an undistinguished crowd among the
" also rans."

And of the main groups that make up the
dolomitic district, I do not think that any can beat
the charm and grandeur of the Pala Range—even
if you left the Cimon outside the reckoning. It is
curious to see how the Dolomites rise round their
centre in isolated blocks of mountain, the coral-reefs
(according to Richthofen's theory) of a day when
earth was yet cooling and all of Europe a sea—the
Pala mass, the range of the Rosengarten, the bulk
of Marmolata and her satellites, the Sella group,
the Tofana group, lonely Pelmo, lonely Civetta, the
long range of Marmarole and Sorapiss, the block of
Cristallo, the Croda, the Drei Zinnen, and, farther
away, the *rudis indigestaque moles* of the Sexten
masses, and the ridges of Gardenazza. In the
middle, round Predazzo, is the centre of the primal
disturbance that the coral islands rose to watch the
grave of; for all the convulsions of Predazzo are
due to the oldest submarine volcano in Europe,
somewhere just beyond where the Monzoni Pass
at present runs—a vomit of subaqueous fire and
fusion compared with which the Grampians and
the Snowdon Range are mere babies, quite late in
their appearance on the liquescent earth. And so

around it, in the fulness of later times, there rose
that series of coral atolls from the warm and placid
sea ; and these, weathered and splintered and worn,
are the Dolomites of to-day.

To the Rolle Pass I would willingly return again
and again and again. Not only because of that
dominating presence overhead, but because of the
ineffable beauties all around it, near and far. For
the views are unsurpassable anywhere, the expeditions endless, over the rocks and the flowery Alps :
and the dear little inn, though small and simple, is
admirably adapted for the comfort of quiet souls to
whom clean simplicity of living is sufficient joy to
ask of any inn. And the flowers are of a richness
to match the views. For on the one side of the
pass you have the dolomite, with all its usual
treasures and several more besides ; and on the
other rises the stern and gaunt igneous ridge which
culminates in Colbricon, towering above its cluster
of little lakes. But you will do well to beware if
you go far upon the range of Colbricon with pencils
about you, for here, as always happens where the
flora is specially thrilling, you will be tight-roping
upon a frontier. I suspect the Kings and Emperors
of the earth to have consulted malignant botanists
when they made their demarcations. Anyhow,

though I have not wandered far enough on Colbricon to meet with any question, I can tell you that
as soon as you are up on the Alp you will find huge
slabs of *Silene Pumilio* tightly sandwiched between
the layers of the rock ; like succulent short turf are
its mats, and then come up those lax rosy flowers
like stemless pinks. When I was there, however,
the season was still so young that round the plants
the swollen baggy seed-vessels of the year before
still lay scattered and full of good seed ; they had
broken off neatly at the neck, and lay so thick
about each tuft that for a long time I thought those
piles of withered bladders must represent the indus-
trious hoard of some marmot or mountain squirrel.
Of both tufts and seed I took toll: but *Silene
Pumilio* is a very difficult plant to deal with ; it has
a tap-root of preposterous length, in the first place,
and much resents mutilation. (One specially fine
mat a foot across and a quarter of an inch high, off
which I was able to prise the whole of its covering
boulder-slab, came up at last with a perfect root-
mass of at least a yard in length.) In the second
place, it objects, I believe, to undue damp ; and
objects, I know, to limestone, with a fanatical
intensity.

I have no doubt that farther along the crests

of Colbricon you would come on Eritrichium and
the other high igneous Alpines. I marked a very
probable ridge, and would have made for it ; but
lunch-time was nearing, and the Silene occupied so
much of my attention that I did not want to scamp
my dealings with it. Eritrichium I had seen so
often, but the Silene never before. Another thing
there was, too, to fill my attention on this ridge.
For here, among the melting snow-patches, the
flower-heads of the Sticky Primrose were appearing
in little blots of bright violet upon the sere brown
turf, and in the sodden hollows wetly gleamed wide
masses of the Fairy Primrose ; some of them, indeed, with such a passion of colour that from afar
I hoped that they must certainly be *P. Floerkeana*,
and ran feverishly down over the rocks to see.
However, one hybrid was clearly there, *P. salis-
burgensis*, occurring quite infrequently, and in
the rather wetter slopes, exactly as I had seen it
on the Kraxenträger. It may be that this particular hybrid is only begotten in places where both
the parents bloom thus early. And yet this can
hardly be the case, as wherever the two species
are found, it is evident that they both start into
blossom with the melting of the snow.

Lower down, returning from Colbricon, I came

upon a beautiful sight in a dank dell, where the Rhododendrons were still withered and brown. This was a little shelf of rock, very densely occupied by a stray colony of *Primula glutinosa*, that was in the full beauty of its flower. Just at eye-level those glorious heads of blossom waved in my face; their colour was of the purest violet, varying here and there to a blue as pure and clear as that of a precious stone or *Primula sapphirina*. And their fragrance in the wintry stillness was soft in my nostrils. There is something about the scent of the Primulas that is specially intoxicating — a note of cleanness, dry sweetness, gentleness. I always seem to see their smell as something powdery and white. It is to me the rendered essence, in another form, of the snowy meal that decks *marginata* and *Auricula*, and our own *farinosa*, and the round, sound eye of *carniolica*.

The flowers on the Rolle Pass were singularly backward. I was there this year on the 17th of June, coming south from regions more northerly, where things had been in a far more moving train; but on the Rolle the grass was still bare and bleached from the winter snows, and everywhere stood up in dark battalions the tight, black buds of *Gentiana verna* that had not yet begun to think of unfurling

their heavenly flags. On the other hand, all the
pale turf round the hotel was set with lavish trumpets of *G. acaulis* in forms so fine as I have never
yet been privileged to see that most variable and,
on the whole, unsatisfactory of plants. (For out
of what local variety, or varieties, the long centuries have built up our beautiful great Gentianella
I cannot say, but certainly it is none of the many
Alpine forms that have gone to the composing of
that empty name, *Gentiana acaulis.*) Too often
the Alpine *acaulis* is an indigo or slate-coloured
ugliness ; such pure and luminous blues as that of
G. Clusii are rarely met with on Alps lower than
the high rocks that *Clusii* affects. What, then,
was my joy to find that the prevailing note on the
Rolle was a real and royal blue : not at all that
blunted tone which so often disappoints one's eye
elsewhere. And here among the type we each of
us found a white variety—and a good, clean white
variety, too ; not by any means the dingy, bad-
papery affair which passes, at large prices, for the
Albino *acaulis* in catalogues.

I cannot adequately express the joy of roaming
through that glorious air, and with such sights as
the Cimon ready to your eye, across the illimit-
able turf, all starred with Gentians, of the Rolle

meadows in June. It is behind the hotel, of course,
on the dolomitic side of the pass, that you have
these dawning fields of flowers at your disposal,
instead of the sere sedge and dingy, rusty Rhododendrons of the granitic. And here, too, now and
then, in stern limestone cliffs, you will see hanging
out the fluffy grey tufts of *Campanula Morettiana*,
tightly wedged into the crevices, and only to be
extracted with wedges and hammer—and only then
at the peril of your life, lest you should bring
down all the rotten and overhanging cliff upon
your head. In the herbage of the lower slopes
there is *Primula longiflora* abounding among
P. farinosa, and wholly refusing to hybridize;
and millions of little dancing pale Soldanellas in
moister hollows, and everywhere regiments of
Gentiana verna, often in forms particularly large
and stout and fine. Then in the cliffs of the
Campanula, so very rare, and only so very difficult
to grow because it is so very difficult to get it out
of the rocks intact to start with, there are also
deep sticky cushions of the little Tyrolean Primrose, thickly jewelled with its big round flowers of
a rather squalling aniline pink. *Primula tyrolensis*,
which seems rather to linger obstinately on the
cold northern faces of Sorapiss, is here riotously

happy and abundant between every boulder, and
squeezed into every cliff-face and ledge and cranny,
whether in sun or shelter.   Its only close relation
is *P. Allionii*, whose habit of growth it follows,
though much smaller in habit, with tiny rounded
leaves, densely sticky, and those very conspicuous and splendid flowers that might so easily
be as perfectly pleasant in colour as *Allionii's ;* but
they have developed more heartiness in their pink,
and heartiness, as often, is here accompanied by
something brazen and second-rate.

Many years ago I used to have inquiries about
a Primula called *P. Juribella*, what it was, and
where it came from.   I was even more ignorant
then than I am now, and I had no notion.   On
ransacking the deepest recesses of my brain, I
could only rake up a wild theory that the name
might have something to do with the Jura, and
the Primula prove prevalent in those parts ; slow
years, however, taught me better than that.   But
I never wholly fathomed the mystery of *P. Juribella* until one day when I was idly conning a
map of the Dolomites and planning a tour ; suddenly my eye was caught by the word " Giuribel."
The riddle of the Primula was solved.   It is called
after the Giurbella Alp above the Val Travignolo,

by the Rolle Pass, for the excellent reason that it is not to be found there at all, to the best of my belief and researches ; for *Primula Juribella* is a hybrid between the Tyrolean and the Fairy Primrose, and is extremely unlikely to be found upon a cow-Alp, where neither of them occurs.

Accordingly I went searching one August along a high rocky ridge of limestone, where *tyrolensis* was abundant in the rocks. I had no idea of where the hybrid was likely to be found, whether with its father, *tyrolensis*, or under the wing of *minima*, its mother. In any case, here was the father, but of the mother there was yet no sign. However, I wandered on until at last I came to a little lap of turf occurring among the rocks, and here, in a moment, I descried the glittering glossy little leaves of *minima*. Now began the struggle—to detect a hybrid without the flower to help. Hunched up almost double, I slowly climbed that slope, and it was not long before I came on leaves rounded at the tip, dark green, with glands inherited from *tyrolensis*, not glossy, but dull in their effect. *P. Juribella* was discovered and collected.

Another year I thought I might as well have a look at her in flower. I returned to the ridge, and *P. tyrolensis* was a rosy sheet in all the rocks, but higher up the hollows of the mountain were filled as yet with snow. However, I persevered through the drifts, and by good luck that one sunny little slope was open, and on it the Primulas were glowing among the wet flattened grass. But *P. Juribella* proved a disappointment; from its father it has taken that shrill note of magenta which is the one fault of *tyrolensis*, while from its mother it has got the ragged outline and thin texture that belongs to the worst forms of *minima*. Had it only kept the shape of *tyrolensis* and the colouring of the best *minimas* it would be a superb treasure; as it was, there was nothing for me to do but to choose out the finest and fattest-formed flowers I could find, and then retire down the side of the mountain, past flowerless silver sheets of *Potentilla nitida*, until I was caught and held spell-bound on the rocky slope by the view of the Cimon, with that white steep bank of débris for foreground.

For clouds were playing tricks that day; now they would sweep the huge pinnacle up from the earth, and make it float in the sky and seem to reel and shiver through the vapours; then they would hide it altogether in a whirling drift of greyness, from which at last would break a gleam of rose, and

then, through the ravelling darkness, the obscurity
would take shape as some wall or promontory; and
then again the mountain would seem to rend and
disperse the veil without an effort, and stand clear
from point to base until some new wisp of vapour
came trailing round, blocking out the mass behind
the foremost spire, and thus making it more spear-
like than before; but soon descending, curling
lovingly about the flanks of bare rock, and growing
and shifting and embracing the peak, until once
again it would be dispersed, and sent back to join
the rolling sea of billows, from behind which now
and then soared looming the vast sword-points and
towers of the Pala di San Martino and the Sass
Maor. So perfectly does the Cimon always play
its part, indeed, that one can hardly avoid the
feeling that he has a keen sense of his own dramatic
value, to which he plays up incessantly with match-
less skill. No cloud is ever allowed in the wrong
place; and if they sometimes cover him altogether,
shall not the star-performer have a right to his rest,
when he must be weary of so indefatigably holding
the finest of all his splendid faces to the public?

CHAPTER IX

AFTER the Rolle Pass I feel it almost a bathos and wholly a tragedy to move on anywhere else. Nor have I ever even had patience to descend upon its farther side to San Martino de Castrozza. Truth to tell, as the truth is so obvious already, I simply cannot bear to leave the high passes, and go down into comfortable fat lands again far from the hills. But for the enormous majority that ask no better, and find the high places austere and uncomfortable, I will add that beyond doubt San Martino is a place of especial charm, and the view that it has of the Pala Dolomites, ragged overhead, must make it well worth staying in for those who do not incessantly crave to be dealing with the Pala Dolomites on terms and levels slightly less unequal.

Meanwhile we will now descend again to Predazzo, and there once more resume our original motor, which continues southward, curving round

by Cavalese and Fontane Fredde towards Bozen.
The way is not thrillingly interesting here, and one
is saddened to say good-bye to the Cima Vezzana
and the Cimon della Pala, as they vanish over
lower intervening wooded ranges. Now we are
careering along a broad upland valley so shallow
and wide and fertile that one has no conception
how high it stands until one reaches its lip over
the valley of the Adige. The road is poorer too,
and altogether there is nothing much to console
one except the fleshpots of Bozen drawing momentarily nearer. You may derive what comfort you can
from a bald building in Cavalese, painted all along
with mitres over the escutcheons of such Bishops
as were armigerent, and blank shields left for such
poor prelates as were self-made. For this was once a
palace of the Prince-Bishops of Trent, and it always
seems to me unfair on the plebeian Bishops to have
their armlessness thus publicly placarded. However,
the slur is not what it was, for the palace of the
Prince-Bishops of Trent has now become a prison.

There is really nothing much to say about the
greater part of the drive down to the Adige. It is
dullish ; and the best thing on the way is the name
Fontane Fredde ; the " Cold Fountains " always
give me a thrill to think of, though when I come

there I find only a stuffy little albergo, and zinc
tables in a garden, and perambulating hens. Then
I remember that Fontane Fredde is also Kalten-
brunnen, and I cease to wonder at the zinc tables,
and am glad to go forward. The last time that I
passed, Fontane Fredde was in a roaring cataclysm
of rain which made the road a creamy river, and
hissed above the throbbing of the motor. We had
had a bad day from the first start out of Cortina.
Only Antelao and Sorapiss had cast the enveloping
clouds from their crests ; on all the other mountains
they lay thick and thicker, with rare glimpses as we
climbed the Falzarego of the great wall of Tofana,
seeming about to fall over upon us through the
mist. On the Pordoi the air grew yet darker and
colder ; we descended to a fresh and magnificent
aspect of the Boe precipices, lurid and black amid
the growing murk. Then as we drove down the
Fassathal we looked behind and saw that the whole
Sella group was by now swallowed up in deep and
violent dark. Soon the same gloom engulfed the
Pala Dolomites also, and the brewing storm pursued
us through Cavalese, and broke at last just as we
were beginning the long and slithering descent into
the valley of the Adige.

So that we missed, this time, the splendour of

that drop. The road goes winding down and down along the face of the huge cliffs that bound the valley of the Adige, until suddenly you see it far down below you, a chequer-board of green vineyards with the river running pale in the middle, past a a long island of porphyry, precipitous and wooded. On the far side of it again rises the rosy rock-wall of the Mendel, and above that, Alp on Alp, until the eye rises to the creamy snowfields of the north and west and south, from the mighty pyramids of the Ortler and the Hochgall to the Adamello and the Brenta and the Care Alto, remote and radiant in the light of morning as you ascend out of the valley on some clear day in June. And then again, the bed of the Adige is such a paradise in itself; from the descent you see its course—up north where the two rivers join, the one coming down from the glaciers of the Ortler, and the Eisak from the Brenner, while at their junction, safe under the shelter of the hill between them, Gries and Bozen sit taking the sun in the warmest corner of the world; and in the south it runs through air perpetually more balmy into colours every moment more blue and golden, past Trent, and Mori, and Rovereto, and under the huge flank of Baldo, pale in the uttermost distances towards Verona.

If you know it in June the celestial valley of the Adige is rich with the unimaginable fragrance of the vine-blossom; all the warm air is laden and thrilling with the sweetness of it; and its mere mention calls up a thousand memories of June— the long descent into Rovereto from Schio, or the exquisite Lago de Toblino, beneath high bluffs of dolomite, lying very calm under the first freshness of a cloudless morning, mirroring its old castle and the shrubs along its winding shore, and clearly revealing the great dark fish that float in its pale waters, so opaquely blue and green; while over all the earth floats in warm waves that scent of the vine in flower. Only less wonderful is the moment when the year is ripening to vintage in the Adige Valley, and a different fragrance vibrates through the air; but by that time dust and heavy heat have replaced the thrilling warmth and the freshness of June, the vines are dark in their green, and the colouring has deepened from the golden blue that fills the distances in spring to something heavier and drier and disillusioned. But at all times the valley of the Adige is indeed an enchanted place, with its high red walls, and guardian peaks, and fertile plains, and little castles perching on points of vantage. And it is the gate of Italy. There is no song in the world so sweet in my ears as the sonorous chant delivered by the station-master on the platform at Bozen, with that thrill and sense of romance which seems the monopoly of the South. And this it is, ringing in my ears always, the promise of fresh life on some hopeless day in the northern winter. " Mori—Riva—Arco—Ala—Verona." Only the names of stations on the way, but try chanting over its music to yourself, and see if it does not vibrate from afar with the call of Italy. Give it full tongue, and unashamed value to all the music of those chiming syllables, then think if the authorities at Euston or St. Pancras could do as much with " Leicester—Sheffield—Leeds—Hellifield—Carlisle—Glasgow." Perhaps they might, indeed, if they chose, in that instance, thanks to Hellifield and Carlisle—names of romance ; but it is certain they don't, nor want to, their main object being to prevent anybody from being able to make out where their train is going to.

So by this time we are down, down, down from the great heights, and even the Cavalese Valley—such a terrible declension from the high passes—is as far over our heads, at the top of a purple cliff, as the Pordoi or the Rolle above Cavalese. Under red precipices, where on the shingle *Silene Armeria* is glowing among the rosy jungles of *Epilobium rosmarinifolium*, we course gladly up along the smooth levels to Bozen, and there arrive at about 7.30 in the evening, supposing us to have had the wild whim of coming right through from Cortina in the day, starting by about 8.30 at the other end of the clock. In that case it is with relief that one feels the motor driving over the cobbled streets of Bozen, and coming to rest at last close to the parish church, by the post-office just beyond the square.

As a rule, upon my travels I am no friend to towns, and avoid them with all my might, but Bozen I love with a singular and enduring passion. No reason is too flimsy to take me to Bozen, from places no matter how remote. It may be merely, as my critics allege, that there I always eat too much. This, indeed, is "dreadful true"; and here is the reason why Bozen had best be taken at the end of one's travels, or at all events before some such strenuous adventure as the traversing of the Antermoja Pass, by means of which one's excesses may be redeemed and made blessed unto one. For I defy anybody born of woman not to do as I do— at least, if he frequent the Hotel Greif, and sit at meals outside in the public square beneath wide trees, and screened from general gaze by a hedge

of Euonymus and flowering Oleanders. Overhead
is the velvet sky, and around you the polite population of Bozen, all at a thousand little round tables
like your own. You order your dinner from a big
card covered with the names of the most stimu-
latingly incomprehensible viands that impel one to
a gambler's recklessness. In the crowd you have
to wait hours, but everything is such fun that you
would not grudge a moment of them, and beyond,
in the square, the band is playing, perhaps, by the
statue of Walter von der Wogelweide, or some
special military orchestra is giving a performance
in the precincts of the Greif itself. Up and down
run the many neat maidens, overborne by stress
of serving, but never losing their heads, or their
coolness, or their tempers. Fräulein Juli, Fräulein
Anni, Fräulein Fanni, how often have I eaten out
of your hands, and may I survive the doing so
often enough to repeat the joy again and again and
again! The main entrance, too, to the Greif is
actually through the enclosure, so that you see all
the new arrivals, which vastly adds to one's entertainment: travel-stained Austrian professors of
immense size, with rucksacks on their backs, and
large wives trailing behind, who look as if they
never walked a yard in their lives, and have just

strolled down from the Schlern or the Antermoja ;
or neat American women, each with ten enormous
trunks, who have been driving luxuriously over the
Bernina and the Stelvio.

To all alike the sumptuous head-porter extends
his charm, and the head-waiter, portly and smiling
and ambrosial as a *lion comique*, carries the weight
of the hotel on his shoulders, prescribing to every-
body, in every language known to man, what they
would most enjoy to eat and drink.   And so, under
his beams, the dinner comes, and, once started,
continues to arrive with precision ; though sometimes one has to sit and see the dainty which one
knows to be one's own cooling gently on the central
table round a tree which acts as a sort of clearing-
house for the foods as they come ; and wildly wails
to busy Fräulein Fanni across the babel.   Meanwhile a little page-child, with the face of a cherub
who has known the world not wisely but too well,
yet "only wants a pair of wings to be a syrup,"
conveys round postcards for your choice, and in
the intervals brings drinks, while flower-women
come to offer Edelweiss.

It may not be generally known that the unfortunate and perfectly respectable Mary Magdalen,
broken-hearted at having been confused with a rather

disreputable person of the same name, retired at
last to a slope above Bozen, there to take off most
of her clothes and lie on the floor in a cave and look
at a skull, as invariably represented in pictures by
painters who desire a pious pretext for practising
on the nude for the spiritual edification of their
patrons. Anyhow, overcome by this concatenation
of misfortunes, Mary Magdalen took at last to
weeping; and of her tears are now made a wine
that glows like amber and tastes like heaven, and
carries her portrait on its delightful broad-bellied
bottles, which have the added charm (from the
bottler's point of view) of containing so very much
less than one would reasonably expect at the price.
Cause Magdalen's Tears to be brought you, cold
in a pail of ice, by the world-worn seraph, and you
will bless my name, and the coins that have been
so profitably expended on the purchase of this
volume.

Indeed, after austerities and solitude in the
mountains, why should not one feel the riotous
joy of streets and lights and food and drink and
human crowds again? My passion for one set of
joys would be wholly wasted if it dulled me to
another; by the keenness of the one is its contrast
intensified. Therefore, shamelessly and confidently

will I bid you revel in the joys of Bozen, daintily eating under the clipped trees in front of the Greif, and watching the crowds go by beneath the wall of the hotel, where runs the current of the passing public without disturbing the throng of feasters, or being disturbed. I do not think that Bozen is quite the same if one stays anywhere but at the Greif. This is the old hotel, with the maturity and calm of an established house. The town is full of enormous brand-new palaces, filled with frescoes and *art-nouveau* decorations. These are magnificent, but they are not old in bottle like the Greif. I painfully know this, and so does everyone else; for the Greif is very frequently full up unless you take precautions beforehand—and this no matter what be the season of the year, seeing that visitors are always alighting on their way north or south to Italy—and then the owners of the Greif, who are also the owners of the other pompous palaces, will put you into one of the newer sumptuosities, among gilding and velvet and splendours. True, they will still allow you to feed outside the Greif (there are actually people who prefer to feed inside at a crowded table d'hôte); but life in Bozen is never quite the same joy, somehow, if you are not living in the profound and ordered ease of the Greif.

The intrinsic attractions, too, of Bozen are mani-
fold for those who have eyes to see, and are not as
an unfortunate small American I met in the motor
from Predazzo, to whom every place on his travels
appeared to be only a thing to be got away from
as soon as possible, and Bozen in particular a dull
little hole where there was nothing to do. Well,
I concede that Bozen is not Monte Carlo; but all
the better for that. Bozen is a very entrancing
little leisurely warm town, half Italy and half
Austria, with the charm of both; there are shops
full of books and Mr. Compton's pictures; there
are long arcaded streets in which one may wander
by the hour scanning the dark windows. Some of
these belong to *Antiquitätenhandlung*, where you
may pass through an old carved door in some
obscure arcade, and suddenly find yourself in a
spacious airy palace of old time, in which every
sort of absurd gimcrack is now piled up to tempt
the passing curio-maniac. Then there is a church
in the Walther Platz, not a stone's-throw from the
Greif, with the most beautiful tower of fretted
stone, and a roof no less beautiful, done in patterns
of green iridescent tiles, till the effect is like some
particularly wonderful lizard. In the outside of
its walls there are inserted knightly headstones

with elaborate armouries, and though the inside be now but dingy and eighteenth-century, you can indulge wholesome feelings, if you will, over the odd notions that keep out for worship anything so horrible as the sere swaddled corpse and bare skull of St. Cœlestinus, martyr. Then there is a small public garden where the currant-red plumes of Lagerstrœmia make the whole waving bush a glory in August, and the Althæas are great trees, all covered with white or pearly flowers among the weeping soft green of Deodar and Cedar, so unexpected in such a neighbourhood and with such companions.

Bozen is always warm, and in summer divinely hot. You sit and eat ices outside the Hotel Walter von der Wogelweider, and between sips ponder what mysterious impropriety is inherent in *Eiskaffee,* that you are never able to obtain it at the Greif or any other really dignified establishment. And then towards sundown you will do well to go up the Virglbahn, a little electric funicular up the steep side of a hill two or three hundred yards away (there is now a yet higher railway, most horrific, whose car runs up over vacancy on a single wire). And here, on its shoulder, is a big restaurant gleaming down

after dark upon Bozen with its countless lamps,
like an illuminated galleon hanging in the air.
And from this point—as, indeed, from almost
anywhere in Bozen, but from here most superbly
—you have a view of the Rosengarten group
aspiring magnificently, splinters and scarps and
spires and battlements of rosy red at sundown.
As you go up to the Brenner from Italy, indeed,
this is the one glimpse of the Dolomites that you
get from the railway ; it ranges from the high table
of the Schlern, through the sword-blades of the
three Vajolet Towers, to the immense mass of the
Rose-garden close beside.   But from the Virglwarte
you get them yet more impressively, and their full
height and volume come out ; there is a little rock
behind the restaurant where grow houseleeks and
dainty small garlics, and a Pratensis Anemone which
apparently never flowers.   Here it is very pleasant
to lie and watch the colours glowing and fading on
the Rose-garden in the intervals of turning towards
the other view from this shoulder into the golden
bluenesses of the Adige Valley. And down at
your feet lies Bozen, nestling under its hill between
converging rivers.   It looks like a toy-thing, and
you feel you could almost throw a stone down
upon the patterned verdure of the church-roof.

Dear Bozen, the mother of sound wines and Magdalen's Tears! Head of the world, too, I am told, in *Obst* export—though by my own experience I must confess that, to my own taste, the fruit with which the Bozen stalls are daily stacked is usually hard and savourless and bullet-like. I do really believe that foreign races have a less exacting standard for table-fruit than ours. How else can it be supposed that the adamantine peaches with which the Continent swarms in summer can ever come to be consumed?

There is yet another railway expedition you may make from Bozen (exclusive of that up to Spondinig, if you mean to go over the Stelvio to Tirano, and thence down to Como and Italy, or over the Bernina into Switzerland), and that is the expedition up to the Ritten and Klobenstein by the Rittnerbahn. This mounts the hill behind Bozen, and passes through the famous vineyard from which Magdalen's Tears are expressed. In autumn all the vineyards are a-twinkle with mirrors hung to scare the birds; and one day from the Virglwarte we were very hard put to it to discover the meaning of those many brilliant points of light that came and went so mysteriously in Magdalena's vineyard. In the end we concluded that they must be flashes from the knives of men gathering the grapes.

The Ritten, to which the railway ultimately attains, is the upper level of the hills above the Adige Valley. Here it unfolds into a wide grassy Alp (corresponding to the Seiser Alp across the Eisak Gorge), which has been turned into a sort of summer suburb for Bozen, the richer residents having each a villa here. Farther on, again, are dreadful things called *Erdpyramiden*—boulders originally lodged on gravel-banks, which have been gradually eroded, except where the boulder protected them; so that now you see a forest of sand-columns, with great blocks of stone, like unwieldy hats, balanced upon their points. The real glory of the Ritten, however, is its unparalleled view right across the valleys upon the Schlern and Rosengarten, now exactly opposite, and unfolded in their fullest splendour. In the autumn evenings, when that huge southern wall of the Schlern goes fiery scarlet, there could be no finer view-point than this. At the same time I do not love the place, and have unfairly allowed my spleen to bubble over upon the interesting *Erdpyramiden*; and I know that unless I here make this prompt apology, I shall get many stern letters rebuking me for having slandered such respectable wonders of Nature. But what would you? After three days amid the delights of Bozen one's appreciation of even *Erdpyramiden* is apt to be dulled by internal causes, and internal causes spoil the best external effects.

CHAPTER XI

THE SCHLERN

If you want to get away from Bozen back into the Fassathal by a new route, you can climb the deep and winding gorge of red rock that leads by Karneid and Welschnofen up to the Karer Pass, and so down upon Vigo di Fassa. Alas, however, you cannot thus climb in a motor, whether public or private; the road is too narrow, and bad, and unimprovable. Therefore you have to take the slow-crawling diligence from Bozen (there are many different services daily, for the Karer See is a celebrated tourist resort), or charter a carriage of your own. The drive is dull, and the method of progression duller still; and therefore it is perhaps that I have no warm words for the Karer Pass. Its best point is that from the great hotel just below its crest you can again take a motor over to Vigo di Fassa on the other side. One climbs endlessly through pinewoods, and so incidentally, and almost unregarding, passes a very small, very clear, green puddle by the roadside ; and then comes into view the fierce ragged range of Latemar over the fir-trees on your right, and on the left all the Rosengarten group in a sweeping wall, with the flat bulk of the Schlern shouldering far out over the valley at the end ; and thus arrives finally at a hotel of monstrous size and splendour and luxury and elaborate woodwork. (The actual pass is higher up, with more hotels peppered along the way.)

I do not like the Karer Pass. I do not like the Karer See. This is wrong of me ; the Karer See is universally acknowledged to be the most beautiful piece of water in the Dolomites. It is the *raison d'être* of that stupendous hotel, positively dolomitic in the irregularities of its roof-lines ; it is the *raison d'être*, too, of all the crowds of large-hatted lovelinesses that in summer throng the lawns with their elaborate frocks. Accordingly, when I arrived at that palace, in solitary charge of the indefatigable aunt, whose belongings were for the moment lost, the first thing we did was to get away from the hotel as soon as possible, and set out in search of that exquisite lake among the pinewoods that so theatrically (according to the

illustrations) mirrors the Latemar in its unruffled
waters. There, we concluded also, should we find
the lost belongings. A little perturbed already in
spirit by their disappearance, we set out. There
were no signposts to direct us to the Karer See,
which was strange; and the two or three tourists
of whom we asked the way looked upon us with
astonished eyes, as if we had asked some question of
doubtful propriety, and merely waved their hands
round the horizon. However, I put this to the
discredit of my defective German, and having
found a path that looked well trodden, we em-
barked upon it, feeling that a broad track, called
"Anna Maria's Way," was bound to lead us sooner
or later to the Karer See.

Laden with the coats and cloaks and Baedekers
of the lost belongings (which the aunt steadfastly
refused to leave behind in the carriage), we trudged
and trudged and trudged along that interminable
woodland path, which showed no sort of sign of
ever arriving anywhere in particular. The day
was hot, the forest stuffy and stifling; we felt it
would be cowardice to turn back, so on we toiled,
dripping like Niobe. Rarely have I detested anything as I then detested Anna Maria. To this
day I conceive that the poor lady must have been

insane; for at last, when our molten legs were
giving under us, we came out upon a small green
hollow of grass, which might at some more fortunate
time have been a pool, seeing that a mouldering
boat lay embedded in the herbage at one end.
This, then, was the illustrious Karer See—a dank
and viewless hollow in the middle of the wood!
We looked at each other with disgusted eyes, and
returned limply along Anna Maria's idiotic Way,
both, by this time, too cross for utterance, even in
commination of the Karer See. I should have
liked to leave those bulky Baedekers to rot in the
boat. However, at last we arrived once more in
front of the hotel, flushed and embittered and
dropping with the fatigue of disappointment; and
there we found the lost belongings tranquilly sitting
on a pile of logs, eating wild strawberries. And
learned that after all our trouble the Karer See
had been that absurd little pool we had passed by
the roadside. A lake, indeed; it is more like a
salt-cellar. Do you wonder if I am jaundiced to
the Karer Pass? As for the aunt, she was so cross
with her restored belongings, no less than with
Anna Maria, that she utterly refused to look at the
strawberries they proffered in propitiation; and
though she ultimately contrived, indeed, to eat the

whole lot, it was in a complete absence of mind,
when nobody was looking, and without the slightest
mitigation of her just displeasures.

The railway takes you from Bozen to the Brenner,
passing up the deep gorge of the Eisak, where the
river, blue and clear as a jewel, tumbles along
under precipices of crimson porphyry. At Blumau
you can alight for Weisslahnbad and the Tierserthal under the southern wall of the Schlern (which
from a few points in the profound gully of the river
is seen appearing above the precipices overhead,
looking stupendous and impregnable). We, however, will continue to the next important stopping-
station : although, indeed, it seems absurd that such
tiny halts should have any importance at all, much
more that the big expresses should honour them
with the courtesy of a stop, until one remembers
the many pleasure-places up above which are thus
fed from the railway.   Our alighting - point is
Waidbruck, whence a carriage-road deviously as-
cends the faces of the cliffs, and winds up through
tunnels and rapid gorges of the red rock until it
emerges on the upper levels. Here there are still
climbs to be achieved, and the road coils upwards
through fields and woods towards Kastelruth,
which one sees awaiting one's arrival high above

upon an eminence.   Kastelruth is a pleasant little
place looking out over all the smiling green lands
that roll at the foot of the Schlern, thick-set with
villages and hotels and churches with chocolate-
coloured bulbs at the top of their spires.   But the
pride of Kastelruth is its view of the Schlern.

For now you are on the upper plateau, and the
huge mountain stands straight in front of you in
all its naked brutality, a mass like a giant's table,
rising up on every side from the forest in one unbroken wall.   And on the extremity that hangs
out over Seis two slices of the mountain have been
split away, and stand up now from the main bulk
in awful twin pinnacles, which when you first
sight them over the pinewoods below Kastelruth,
are as startling as, and form an even more perfect
picture than, the Cimon from the Rolle Pass.   And
yet what a ridiculous little thing in reality is this
enormous Schlern that here from Kastelruth fills
half the world, and from Seis to Salegg blocks it
all with its impending peaks and the vast splendour
of its wall.   When you see it from the Belvedere or
the heights about the Pordoi, you look down, down
upon it far under the last tail-end of the mountains,
and this huge giant's table, as it seems from Kastelruth or Bozen, becomes a little toy campstool at a

child's tea-party. However, one can only judge one's friends, whether among men or mountains, by the present standards available ; and at this point the Schlern appears as gigantic in its monopoly of size as a tolerably presentable man appears a model of brilliance in the company of the wholly unregenerate, or the smallest jest at a parish tea.

After Kastelruth the road becomes rapidly worse (no motors are allowed up any part of it) and dips towards Seis, a big, pleasant, scattered town of villas and pensions and summer hotels lying dotted about in the wide meadows under the Puflatsch, a dull, but from here imposing, bulk of granite (the home, therefore, of *Saxifraga Aizoon* in abundance) that fronts the Schlern and supports the tableland of the Seiser Alp. All this district is a little too smooth and pleasant and populous for my own taste. It is the *Sommerfrisch* of countless governesses and nice maiden ladies who enjoy German comfort, and like to sit about in green meadows, with impregnable mountains making a pretty background to the picture. Salegg, in especial, which squats under the shadow of the Schlern, a mile or so (by a divergent road) from Seis, consists wholly of a huge hotel consecrated to summer-pensioners, among whom are counted

Kings. None the less, I cannot glow towards the Salegg; all that life seems to me illegitimate, and I object to having my mountain views obliterated by the feathered hats of women, no matter how illustrious and obese.

The main view which the Hotel Salegg fronts is too pretty-pretty and bland, I confess, for my rugged personal taste. You are allowed no guess at the height you have gained; you get no glimmering suspicion of the Eisak Valley lying beyond those trim meadows some thousands of feet below; you might be anywhere about sea-level for all those rolling pastures and smooth fat lines of field convey; and the snow-masses of the Adamello and the Ortler only just appear over the green rim, and somehow are neither impressive nor convincing above that vast billiard-table foreground. And on its real view the Hotel Salegg firmly turns its back, for while the Feathers are lying about in the fields, or making a forest at meal-times on the terrace in front, straight over the hotel behind shoots up like the finger of a god the stark glory of the Santnerspitze, the foremost of the two great spires that have broken away from the mass of the Schlern. Nothing is more magnificent in the Dolomites than this wonder in the backyard of the Salegg. You stand with a crick in your neck, or lie at ease under some tree, to look up above the steep fall of the forest to that grey and pink needle, so close over your head that it seems as if it might descend at any moment and crush the Salegg out of existence. Close behind is the Euringerspitze, and then behind that again the naked riven bulk of the Schlern, which here is cloven into a deep ravine between precipices of 2,000 feet, right into the heart of the mass. And all this gaunt and rosy wonder impends upon your unconscious shoulders while you are taking tea on the terrace, and babbling of the green fields that lie unfolded in front of you.

It is plain that I cannot appreciate the many joys and comforts of Seis and Salegg. Indeed, for some reason I have never managed to be really happy anywhere on this side of the Schlern, and I hope I may never have to go there again. But this, it must be understood, is merely a Doctor-Fell feeling of my own, which not the utmost efforts of reason can overcome. I know that all this country is singularly beautiful, that the views of the Schlern are marvellous, that the hotels, and especially the Salegg, are such that the tired traveller says " Ha ! ha !" when he comes within their gates ; and yet I do not like any of it in my heart of hearts. My feelings, though, can be no rule for better regulated tastes, and therefore I smother my own personal antipathies, and repeat that this district and its hotels make the Dolomitic Mecca of every really sensible person. The walks, it will be obvious, are of the utmost comfort, for unless you are a fly to scale the wall of the Schlern, your time can only be filled with pleasant ramblings along its feet. There is one real expedition only from the Salegg, and that is up into the heart of the Schlern Klamm, the deep rift in the mass of the mountain immediately above the hotel. This walk has the advantage of being far too steep and arduous and hot for the Feathers ; in the depths of the Klamm you may be sure of a solitude unattainable elsewhere in the country of Seis.

And here I have no scruple in telling you that among other marvels you will find *Campanula Morettiana* and *Phyteuma comosum*, and *Saxifraga Burseriana* and *Asplenium Seelosii.* I have no scruple, I say, because all these (except the Saxi-frage, which occasionally seeds down into softer places, and is not common, anyhow, so far as I could find) grow always and only in the very hardest rock of those sheer walls, and are absolutely inextricable by the utmost craft or violence of man. But it must be a glad sight, anyhow, and a noble reward for the climb, to see either the wide white moons of the Saxifrage crowding over their silvery, spiny cushions in the early year, or the deep violet bells of the Campanula floating out in late summer from the soft grey masses of its tufts in the stark and shady faces of the precipice. The Saxifrage, too, is here, as always in these parts, that large and lavish form of the Tridentine Alps, or Alps of Trent, which has of late been sent out into the world by a ludicrous mistake under the impossible name of Tridentata (for Tridentina). And this has given birth to *magna* and *gloria*.

Return we now from Salegg to Seis, or else take the easy wood-lane walk that leads round from Salegg to Ratzes, through the pine-forest along the foot of the Schlern, and past the little ruined castle of Hauenstein (or at all events some kindred little ruin perched upon a rock). By either way—but that through the forest is more pleasant, though only for foot-passengers, while from Seis up to Ratzes the carriage-road continues getting steadily worse—one comes at length to Bad Ratzes, the last end of the valley, in a deep obscurity between the Schlern and the Puflatsch. I take a vindictive delight in the name of Bad Ratzes; it so exactly expresses my opinion of the place. I may be unjustly cold about beautiful Salegg and Seis, but I have an even keener dislike for Bad Ratzes, which I have the further satisfaction of justifying by reason. For the place—which consists almost wholly of a bath-house and hotel, where you go for cures in warm mineral waters— sits in a profound, dark, and narrow groove, far down among spruce-forests, black as night. There is no view whatever, there are no pleasant walks, there is nothing to do at Bad Ratzes except go away quickly.

The Frommerhaus, however, is a small hostelry far above Bad Ratzes, on the edge of the Seiser Alp, to which a visit may profitably be made. It is not a big establishment, and looks like a toy châlet, and has a proprietor so very languid about you, and elegant in his demeanour, that one feels it is only by condescension that one is allowed to stay there at all. However, the effort of achieving a welcome is worth the trouble. The Frommerhaus, perched on the rim of that great height, has a really stupendous view of the whole Schlern, across the deep valley of darkness below, with

the Euringerspitze and the Santnerspitze magnificently standing forward ; and behind go rolling far
and wide the lavish undulations of the Seiser Alp.
This is the second level of the mountains above the
Eisak Valley, the fields of Seis being the first, and
the flat crown of the Schlern the third ; and then
on that triply rising pedestal at last begin the real
mountains. The Seiser Alp has the further
distinction of being the largest Alp in any
European mountain-range—that is, the widest
extent of Alpine pasturage and hayfield. I am
told that in flower-time it is a spectacle of bewildering beauty, waving in sheets of colour to the
horizon, and from what I have seen there of seed-
vessels I should well believe this to be true, though
at the time of my own visits the Seiser Alps,
largely mown and swept and garnished, have had
rather a depressing effect in the first declining
moments of the summer.

On the other hand, I can with difficulty imagine
a more delightful place for a long stay in early
summer than the Frommerhaus. Every day you
could have a different ramble over acres of Geum,
Gentian, and Anemone in every direction, and
always in front of you, facing southwards, the
splendour of the Schlern ; while to the north, across

the far reaches of the Seiser Alp and the topmost shallows of the Grödenthal, you have the glorious masses of our old friends the Langkofel and the Plattkogel, more dominant than even from the other side above the Fassathal. For here the Langkofel stands out over the meadows and valleys like a vast and rugged castle, while on the near side the Plattkogel shows the long smooth slope that earns its name. Beyond these again are the ranges of the Gardenazza Dolomites, and the Hohe Tauern, remote and snowy in the north; while to the left, far away across the invisible and unguessable depths of the Eisak, shine the snowy pyramids of the Brenner, the Oetzthal Alps, the Ortler, the Zillerthaler group, the Presanella, the Care Alto, and the Brenta—a tremendous intermittent wall of snow-peaks, from the Hochgall in the north to the Cima di Brenta away in the south, in the golden country of Garda. But above everything is that view of the Langkofel, unquestionable and imperial as it has not room to be upon its narrow perch above the Fassathal. Here it has room to swell and develop its proportions, with a real valley to itself sloping away from the stone-wastes at its feet, past St. Christina and St. Ulrich in Gröden, where all the Christmas toys of the world are carved. Here come as many summer-visitors as frequent the kindred luxuries of Seis or Salegg, coming up also from Waidbruck. The best of all points for this view is from the summit of Puflatsch, which had looked so high and imposing from Seis, but is from the Frommerhaus only a gentle stroll up various flowery slopes to a flowery summit. Beyond it, on the farther side, is the village of Pufels, which merely inspires me with the comment that this district is unfortunate in its ideas of euphony. How hard to twine a tender feeling about such noises as Pufels, Ratzes, and Puflatsch!

The direct way up the wall of the Schlern, however, does not diverge by the Frommerhaus, but goes directly up the steep Touristensteig, climbing towards the higher levels of the Seiser Alp, exactly in the notch of the stream-gorge, where the Alp curves round to the Schlern. The path mounts steeply but not unpleasantly through the woodland, every step taking you farther from Ratzes and into closer quarters with the Schlern, whose façade is drawing momentarily nearer, and looking momentarily higher. Ultimately you reach the end of that first climb, and find yourself at the friendly but simple inn of the Prossliner Schwaige,

hanging on the edge of the upper plain, and looking straight down upon the groove of darkness in
which Ratzes lies undiscoverably buried. At the
Prossliner Schwaige you can have food and drink at
your pleasure, and perhaps a bed ; but it is best to
push straight on, I think, up the Schlern, whose
wall is now very close overhead on the right, and
looking much more near and negotiable than before.
I left the Salegg at a comfortable hour in the
morning, and by four or five, after a delicious,
leisurely day, was on the top of the Schlern ; for I
am no friend to earlier starts than need be, and I
specially love to lounge and linger by the way. I
am told that mountaineers abhor this method, and
declare that it gives no rest. In my own experience it does—thanks, no doubt, to the incorrigible
eccentricity of my nature ; and up a mountain-side
I like to go in rapid runs, with intervals of sitting
down to pant and hang out my tongue and con-
template the glories of the unfolding world. And
at the end I am certainly no less bobbish than the
well-trained people who continue always grinding
steadily onwards and upwards with their noses to
the path.

After the Prossliner Schwaige the path bends
round the little valley in a curve, crosses the

stream, and then begins to ascend the sides of the
Schlern in long zigzags. The opening distances in
the north are marvellous as one mounts, but the
greatest marvel of all is that here one should be,
after so little time and sweat of climbing, more
than half-way up a mountain that from Seis or
Ratzes looks as if it would take an eagle best part
of the day to reach the summit. The shelving
cliffs on this face of the Schlern, however, have
never yielded me anything very interesting in the
way of plants ; all the usual things are here, but
nothing more. This, though, is not to say that
the general display is not rich and dazzling ; only
that there is no caviare to tickle the appetite jaded
with Gentians. However, as you approach the
top, the show becomes rich enough even for me.
The path tops the great wall, and comes out
upon such another vast undulating field as is the
Seiser Alp nearly 3,000 feet below. And here,
even in late summer, the short grass is thickly
carpeted with flowers : *Potentilla nitida* is in
sheets of pink upon its sheets of silver in stony
places, and Flannel Flower springs everywhere like
Daisies, in such plebeian abundance that one laughs
again at the pretensions of this silly pretty weed to
Alpine rank, and marvels at the sentimental non-

sense that has clothed a thing so facile and common
with a romantic glamour, and surrounded it and
made it sacrosanct with societies for the *Schutz der
Edelweiss*.   However, its grey flannel stars go well
with the roseate loveliness of the Potentilla, and
when all that wide lawn is a rolling surf of Spring
Gentian, Mealy Primrose, Long-Throated Primrose,
Fairy Primrose (this I did not see here, but it is
reported and seems probable), golden Geum, golden
Androsace, vernal Anemone, rue-leaved Buttercup,
it must be more beautiful than most carpets one is
ever privileged to tread.

Not yet are we quite at the Schlernhäuser.   To
one side of that down there rises a further boss, and
on that again a little final pyramid, all a tumble of
stones.   We quietly climb over loose stones and
cliffs curtained with the pink and silver of the
Potentilla, and then, just over the shoulder, come
upon the Schlern-houses, nestling beneath the last
ascent.   This is my best-beloved club-hut, after
the Capanna Monza.   It is a long, low building
with a high, vaulted dining-room, from which you
look out into the whole of the Rosengarten range,
now quite close at the end of the neck of rock that
makes the Schlern a peninsula and not an island.
They are wonderful, those huge domes and pin-

nacles, ranging along the world in a battlemented
wall, until at their far end they drop away upon
the Karer Pass, to rise again on the other side in
the jagged hedge of the Latemar. They are
wonderful from the windows of the Schlern-houses,
but even more so from the actual summit of the
Schlern, a desolation of broken limestone blocks,
perhaps some twenty minutes or less above the
hotel. For then, over the Rosengarten range and
the hills beyond, you have your first sight of the
fierce southern face of the Marmolata, which comes
with a shock of surprise to all those who have only
known the mountain on its enormous but comparatively unimpressive northern side. For on
the south she falls away in one vast precipice to
her base; of the snowfield you can only see a
shallow dome. Her shape is that of a right-angled
triangle standing on one of its shorter sides. Imagine
you are looking along the rind side of the melon-
slice in your plate, or, even better, imagine one of
those old slant-lidded steep stationery cases of last
century, according to Churchill's inspired simile,
borne amply out by his fine drawing of it from the
Sasso di Damm. The effect is stupendous; one has
hardly eyes for Pelmo peering over the farthest
ridges, and looking from here like a huge eagle

brooding sullenly. As for the view in the south, you are looking down the whole of the Adige Valley, and your gaze is arrested only by the films of uttermost distance, where Baldo, hardly discernible, walls in the Lake of Garda. Almost at your feet, too, the precipice shrinks abruptly towards the Schlern Klamm. Climb carefully a little, and you will be on the edge, looking straight into that awesome ravine down upon the Salegg, lying like a châlet among the dark fur of the forest.

On these stark walls I suppose it is that one might find *Androsace Haussmanni* if one dared, for the plant has been reported here. As for the other record of the Schlern summit, *Eritrichium nanum*, I have always been deeply sceptical, and not even the botanist's plea that it is now exterminated will wholly persuade me that it was ever found here at all. For is not this white Schlern summit of the limiest limestone? and when was Eritrichium ever found on such? However, another learned botanist wanted me the other day to find Eritrichium in certain limestone crags of the Karawanken, and when I howled my incredulity, protesting that I had never seen Woollyhair on the limestones, replied that he himself had never seen it anywhere else. None the less, there also he had

to confess that it had been exterminated (by himself, he dared to own), and was no more to be seen.
My suspicions are not lulled. That learned one
was well acquainted with all the Alps, and must
have visited a thousand igneous peaks. Am I
really to believe that he had never seen Eritrichium
luxuriating on them? For of that, at least, I am
certain—that there it is, despite my friend; that it
does there exclusively luxuriate in the main chains,
even though I have since heard confirming state-
ments that there *is* a calcareous Eritrichium-form
in the Eastern Alps. Yet, until I have with my
own eyes beheld a limestone crag be-turquoised by
Eritrichium, I shall have to continue believing that
the King of the Alps, in decent and normal form,
is unalterably faithful to the fire-born rocks; but
I will keep an open mind on the point, as well as
an open eye.

CHAPTER XI

THE Schlern runs back, I say, in a long spit of upland, to join the long range from which he stands forward at a right angle over the bed of the Eisak. A high spine of grey and rosy rocks, culminating in the brilliant russet of the Roterdspitze, and ending in the Red Teeth—a long series of russet jags—is the connecting band, and along it, descending to the saddle at first, and then mounting again by degrees, runs the marked track that takes us from the hut, on the last and most glorious of all our rambles, through the very heart of King Laurin's Rose-garden. On my first adventure in that direction I was beaten back. We sallied forth from the Schlern-houses gaily, and mounted the ridge to the point where the path drops suddenly over the southern edge; and there, in rotten and dangerous rock, among red Julias of a hairiness inconceivable, we found, for the first time in my

178

Dolomitic experience, fat green cushions and
sponges of *Androsace helvetica*, a plant of such
great elevations that I have but rarely seen it in
these parts (indeed, the only other place where I
recall it is hanging out in sickly tufts, as becomes
a calcareous plant compelled to dwell among volcanic tents of Kedar, upon the black walls of the
Padon Chain). Along the cliffs, however, below
the Roterdspitze, the plant is abundant, though
hard to get. In the excitement of scrambling
among the collapsing pinnacles, and gingerly
adventuring down some shingle-shoot whose end
could be seen 2,000 feet below, we lost count of
time, and forgot to notice the growing darkness.
Suddenly we looked up, to find ourselves in a lost
world of swirling obscurity, and in the same moment
sounded the roll of thunder. We regained the
ridge, clinging to the red marks of the path. (And
here I will pause, amid the gathering storm, to say
how admirable it is that every one of these Austrian
mountain-tracks is clearly and unmistakably marked
at every few yards with splashes of red or blue or
yellow on the rocks—painted on both sides, too,
so that neither going nor coming can you possibly
lose your way ; and the sign-posts at starting mark
each possible destination with the colour of its own

path, so that you can suffer no confusion as to your
direction.)   By this time. however, the whole ridge
was swathed in deep cloud, every instant growing
denser and more murky.   There was nothing for
us but to return as fast as we could towards the
Schlern-houses.

But in another moment the storm was on us;
and the thunder crackled over our heads and round
our very feet in an incessant series of arid, rattling
shots.   Our trowels hummed with the electric
excitement.   I was glad we had no ice-axes to
draw the mountain-doom upon our heads.   Through
the flickering fires of the lightning we trotted
onwards, and the thunder shouting round us was
a nearer neighbour than I like.   Dense darkness
occupied the mountain, and only those red splashes,
so close together that no fog could hide them,
remained to remind us of track or direction.   And
then through the booming thunder came the hail,
carried on swift wings by the wind that swept the
ridge.   And oh my goodness, how it hurt!   Driven
almost horizontal by the storm, it cut and stung
like whips, full in our faces, and smacking through
one's thin breeches with the smart of a birch.   We
pulled our hatbrims over our eyes as low as possible,
and ran along that ridge as best we could, jumping,

tumbling, stumbling among the stone-slides, and over the ghostly wastes of limestone gleaming wan in the darkness, lit by the flicking, wavering blue fire out of the clouds. It was a miracle that neither of us sprained his ankle. Huddling our clothes as close about us as we could, we ran and ran against that fury, uttering little cries of anguish from time to time beneath the sting of some especially outrageous onslaught; and when at length, breathless and whipped scarlet all over the front of our bodies, we tottered into the benign warmth of the Schlern-houses, that hailstorm ceased immediately, and gave place to snow.

All that afternoon it steadily snowed. We changed, and sat, warm and fed and comfortable, in the big dining-room, looking out upon the falling whiteness. Then, towards evening, the cloud thinned and scattered and broke. A little while and the sky was clear and blue as if it had never snowed or rained at all, and the sun was shining through the wet air upon a glistening world of white. All the Schlern was covered as if it had been midwinter, three inches deep or so; and on the Rosengarten range in front of us fresh whiteness lay wherever whiteness could lodge on those fearful cliffs and spires. But the beauty of their colour was a joy for which one would hardly, afterwards, have grudged one's body naked to the whips of the hail. All the noble peaks and domes of the Rose-garden were of a lucent violet-blue through the moist air—a rich depth and solemnity of colour that I have never seen before or since, deep, diaphanous, and pure; their lines stood opulently out against the delicate pale blues of the sky behind.

Down into Italy had passed the storm; the broken wreckage of the clouds lay here and there among the far-off mountain-ranges, floating in little woolly rolls of gold among peaks and crests of the palest and most transparent azure, which rose among them like islands from some billowy sea. The blue of the mountains varied down into the distance, from the profound and liquid sapphire of the Latemar, out into the further and further unfoldings of the sunshine, through deeper blues and soft violets to paler and clearer and paler, and all of them liquid as something seen through water, till the eye rested at last on Baldo and the hills of Garda, perfectly distinct, yet thin and lucent in their vanishing azure as a vision of some early saint in Italy. And in among the ranges lay everywhere those puffs and undulating beds of

harmless cloud glowing softly golden in the sun.
And the whole Adige Valley lay gilded green and
blue beneath them in a powdery haze of colour
and slanting universal light, to where it gently
melted out of view in the fainting sapphires of the
south. Of the high snows and how they looked
that day I cannot speak—the Brenta, the Care
Alto, the Ortler; they may have been hidden by
the summit of the Schlern. I doubt it though.
But my eyes were wholly chained to the radiant
and unearthly beauty of that prospect down the
valley of the Adige, broad and placid and luminous
in peace after the storm, with Bozen snugly lying
at our feet, visible at the junction of the rivers.

My next adventure into the Rosengarten range
was taken a year or two later, and met from first
to last with no mishap. From the Schlern-houses
we started again upon the Grasleiten path, up
along the ridge, and then abruptly down under
and along the cliffs where the Androsace hangs
out its fluffy green domes. The day was glorious,
and we lingered nowhere, not even among the
noble tufts of *Gentiana angulosa*, that glorified
verna which abounds along the Schlern, nor among
the little breasts all covered with the citron-yellow
jasmine-blossoms of *Androsace* (*Douglasia*) *Vita-*

liana, which there carpets the ground : nor even among those open earthpans on the crest which are filled with tiny rounded knubbles of glossy metallic stuff, very heavy and most mysterious. We made straight along the track, which continues downwards under the precipices, and in and out of the gorges through which the stone-shoots fall away to the Tierserthal, microscopic down below. After a brief interval of paying our respects to the Androsace, we continued dropping quickly below the ascending levels of the Roterdspitze overhead, and making directly for a wide notch in the wall of the Rosengarten range, now quite close in front. This leads up over the Tierser Alpl Joch to the Molignon Pass, while round an outstanding buttress of dolomite farther to the right runs up the narrow gorge of the Grasleiten Pass between the Grasleitenspitze and the Great Valbuon. This was our direction ; and though on arriving in the range we wandered for a time up the Tierser Alpl Joch towards the Molignon Pass, we found the flowers of no special interest, and so returned again to the divergence of our path, where the Grasleiten track wastes labour most dreadfully by descending down and down and down over the most breakneck precipices into the abysses of the Bärenloch,

only to mount up all that lost height again on the
other side of the big buttress, and thus climb
fiercely up and round a steep shoulder over into
the narrow groove of the Grasleiten Gorge. However, the toil repays itself; for nothing can be more
impressive than to pause in the smooth and rocky
gloom of the deep Bärenloch, and look up above
you to the path, far overhead, by which you have
descended under the tremendous rosy series of
precipices hanging impregnable from the sky from
the invisible heights of the Roterdspitze, which
from the Schlern had seemed so insignificant a
spicule. Clinging among the cliffs comes the path
you have been following; sheer blank walls fall
away below it, and rise in thousands of stark feet
above. One feels infinitesimal in the jaws of the
Bärenloch, gazing humbly up at cliffs so huge and
inaccessible.

Then one turns to make good lost ground, and
under the projecting bastion which the Grasleitenspitze throws out over the Tierserthal, we toil
and mount and scramble up the little narrow valley
round the corner. Gradually we climb above the
herbage, and the glen becomes a gorge of bare
grey stones. And here on the slope, as it were
wedged in between gigantic mountains, sits the

Grasleiten Hut.   Starting comfortably from the
Schlern we arrived in time for lunch; ate and
were refreshed for an afternoon of sauntering in
the amphitheatre of stone slopes that, up behind
the hut, descend on all sides from the vast mountains close around.   It is a wonderful place this,
only fitted for those who are strong enough to
bear Nature at her very grandest and most austere.
There are no amenities in the heart of the Rose-
garden: vast domes rise up into the blocked
heaven above precipices of naked rock, and from
their base long slides of stone descend to the
shingly waste at the centre where the stream has
its birth, trickling from the snows that lie banked
on the Molignon Pass to one side and the Grasleiten
Pass to the other.   Pass, indeed, is too high a
name to give these mere notches between the
mountain pyramids round that wild basin.   The
Molignon comes over under the Antermojakogel
on the north, and the Grasleiten climbs to the
south under the colossal shadow of the Kesselkogel.   Endless slopes of snow they were that
August, and the track of travellers was a little
dotted line down their middles.   Nowhere does one
feel more free from the pettinesses of man than
amid the lonely and annihilating splendours of that

place. No matter how many be the crowded tourists ascending or descending, they seem to vanish and be absorbed by its immensities, leaving you alone to face the crushing and uplifting desolation of that rock-bound silence.

So enormous is the barrenness and glory of that stony caldron that it takes one time to notice that even here there is a sign of life. For over the shingle everywhere lie the fragrant lilac tuffets of *Thlaspi rotundifolium*, and though this plant is universal in the highest dolomitic shingles, I have never seen it, either in the Dolomites or anywhere else, so fine in form, so abundant, so comfortable and compact and robust in habit, as here in the silt above the Grasleiten Hut. These are King Laurin's Roses—these pink cushions of sweetness. I toiled among them for hours, revelling in their scent and beauty. I set my young brother a-toiling, too. It was not long before he fell to reviling Iberidella (for so I always think of the plant, by its superseded but much prettier and more expressive name). In the end he called it Vituperata, and loudly cursed it. For Vituperata—has any gardener ever called it that before, I wonder?—has a long tap-root diving naked into the shingle, and needs care in its extraction unless you are as prac-

tised as I in levering out the whole thing with
your stick in one movement from the fine Alpine
shingle. My brother, however, showed great guile;
he would toil with an immense air of industry,
groaning at intervals, or emitting curses, so that I
was filled with a conviction of his unfeigned energy.
And in the end, when I went to look, I would find
after an hour of such work some half-dozen poor
little Vituperatas lying on the bottom of his tin, to
match the loaded, crowded box that was weighing
down my own shoulders.

For here, indeed, is a place where the most
scrupulous need not shy at a hundred plants removed. Remove millions and still the show would
be the same, so abounding is the display of Thlaspi
in that wide amphitheatre of stone slopes up behind the Grasleiten Hut. And then, as we were
wending our way back to dinner, I suddenly halted
in the premature gloaming (for the mountains
close on either side cut out the daylight in
which the rest of the world is still basking), and
gave tongue in cries that re-echoed from the walls
of rock above. For there, seeded down by some
happy chance into the river pebbles, were large
tufts of Haussmann's rare Androsace, far larger
and stouter than it ever grows in the sheer preci-

pices that are its home. This is a plant of the highest dolomitic limestone in the Eastern Alps, found only at great elevations, and then in cliffs so blank that it is usually impregnable. My brother, having learned to know it, and never failing to recognize a plant once seen, subsequently brought it me down from the peak of the Croda da Lago and the Great Zinn. It seems, indeed, almost endemic in the loftiest cliffs of the Dolomites, and is a promisingly beautiful thing when you come upon its masses of soft grey, spidery rosettes, each enclosing the roseate round pearl of a flower-bud. Thus it was in the Grasleiten shingles. I rejoiced over it and greatly loved it. But when I saw its opened flower next day, I came back upon my raptures, for it is not so fat and large as the bud promises, nor quite big enough to make an effect upon the plant ; the colour, too, seemed a thinnish white. Add to which that it is little, if at all, less exacting than the other rare treasures of its exalted section, in which the two friendliest, as I have always found, are *pubescens* and *helvetica.* And ultimately, as I will tell you, I came upon it growing by chance in a very plebeian place, that quite took the edge off its glamour as an inaccessible glory of the cliffs.

So we returned to the Grasleiten Hut, and ordered our dinner. This is the trial that ultimately comes to lie heaviest on one's nerves in the Alpine huts. Sooner or later, after a long course of dinner-ordering, I develop a craving to have my unasked food planked down in front of my unconsulted acquiescence. One of the deepest joys about the Grand Hotel Misurina is that there at last one comes to the luxury of a regular and unalterable *menu*, with which the consumer has nothing to do except eat through the course of dishes that it offers. My brain soon flags over the task of deciding between the comparative merits of meats that I uniformly dislike. The card of possibilities is offered you, and you have to struggle with the choice of *Kalbsfleisch*, *Rindbraten*, *Rostbraten*, *Kaiserfleisch* (a peculiarly revolting preparation of ham in thick slices), *Gulyasch* (Irish stew), and hens in various forms, until my vegetarian conscience becomes strongly reinforced by my jaded appetite and energy. Still, however, the admirable miracle remains, whether you like such meats or no, that such a luxury of selection can be managed in a bare little club-hut some 8,000 feet or so in the heart of the wildest mountains known to Europe.

And then there are always innumerable preparations of eggs after all to fall back upon ; and, in the end, and in this neighbourhood, the comparatively expensive seductions of *Bozener compot*. For be it known that these various items are priced separately in the ultimate bill (a reckoning ludicrously small), and that while ordinary *compots* of plums and cherries, such as are eaten in Austria with every meat-course, are very cheap, the special Bozen mixture comes at least twopence dearer. But the extra outlay on a *Bozener compot* is amply justified, for it gives you all the excitement of gambling, in addition to that of food. For you never can tell what you are going to get in a *Bozener compot*, which is a collection of nearly all the fruits that are known to man, or in any case grown in these parts. Cherries, peaches, greengages are staple articles, and only count one in the game ; but you may get a fig or an apricot, and reckon six ; while it is even possible that you may mark ten, and sail out winner with a black compoted walnut, or a green almond with its kernel still inside.

Alas ! when I woke the next morning, all was wet cloud, and against the gleaming grey walls of the Great Valbuon just outside my window across the gorge, snowflakes were driving thick and fast in the gloom. And nothing else of the mountain world was visible. Clearly our wonderful day over the Antermoja Pass and down again into the Fassathal on the other side was fated never to come off. We waited through the morning sadly, pent in the Grasleiten Hut, beguiling time with the comic papers and Alpine club journals with which all these huts are furnished; and meanwhile wet, mournful tourists came and went, and steamed by the stove, and prognosticated gloom. However, from the bitter cold of the air, and the fact that snow was shining ghostly overhead (whenever the drifting mists allowed one to look up and see dim heights above, pale in the luminous and whirling dark), I gathered a little hope, and we waited on, instead of plunging despairfully down upon Weisslahnbad. Rarely, however, have I seen a more ill-omened-looking day; and it was only in a final bluff that I ran the hours at our disposal as fine as possible, and ordered lunch at half-past eleven, on the last chance of matters then improving. By half-past eleven the rain and sleet had ceased; by twelve the clouds had vanished and the day was glorious.

We sent on our knapsacks by a carrier to await us at Campitello; and in our own good time set out rejoicing. All the stones were wet and glistening as we went up the track that leads from the hut into the wide amphitheatre where the passes go different ways ; and the flowers were nodding and heavy with moisture. Arriving in the amphitheatre we turned to the right, and struck up the long, long snow-slope that climbs to the Grasleiten Pass. It seemed an endless toil, but the snow was in beautiful condition for walking if you chose to keep in the track. But those who were superior and tried to make short cuts were very soon bogged to their knees. Thus, in due time, under the huge cliff of the Kesselkogel, we reached the crest of the pass, and found ourselves looking down the curve of the Vajolet Valley ; while to our left, again, straight up round the corner by the southern wall of the Kesselkogel, the Antermoja Pass went labouring up a snowfield steeper and longer than the last.

On that crest we loitered among the Thlaspis, sweetly mauve in all the open shingles. And here we are in the very heart of King Laurin's Rose-garden. The Rosengarten itself is hardly a stone's throw away now, and by its side are the twisted spears of the Vajolet Towers, and the narrow rampart of King Laurin's Wall. Every peak and turret was clear as crystal in that mountain light. At one point splintered boulders have so fallen as to form a little window on the ridge. As you mount towards the Antermoja Pass (instead of going on down to Perra by the Vajolet Valley), the prospect of that wonderful desolation, here so intimately known and grasped and assimilated, becomes every moment more wide and high and overpowering. The walls, cornice, and crest of the Rose-garden seem to grow as you move, and the angry spears of the Vajolet Towers to menace and waver in the quiet sunlight. But here in this fastness of the Elf King, the Dolomites take for the most part a more solemn and sumptuous note : fewer hairy Julias rise ; the massive bulks, the Rosengarten, Kesselkogel, Antermoja, Seekogel, all clustered round the head of the Vajolet Valley, assume the form of monstrous humps and rounded dominating domes of rock, falling away in sombre precipices stark and grey on every side. And the high desolation of the Vajolet Valley is their heart or aorta, curling down into the far profound gulf of the Fassathal.

The Antermoja Pass is the highest point we have yet reached—over 9,000 feet—and incomparably the most savage and inspiring. The air is silent as a crystal ; the solitude as hard and clear as diamond. It is almost impossible to speak up

there, so wonderful and awful is that enormous
calm in the core of the Dolomites. It seems
either as if one's mortal voice could not be heard
among those other tremendous utterances so vocal
in the great stillness; or as if one's chirp would
shatter beyond hope of repair something gleaming
and holy and incomprehensible. Each soul can
render only to itself alone the particular mystery
and sacrament it gathers from such a scene; for
myself, I know no place where one can draw deeper
or more lasting breaths of enlargement and purifi-
cation than among the crowded presences, the
vibrating breathless emptiness of the Antermoja,
so full of awe, so unimpeding to the winged
expansion of the spirit. I am sorry if I may seem
rhapsodic; a reputed critic once said of some such
remark of mine that it was not "the real thing." I
should be sorry indeed to be thought insincere, but
adequacy here is not within the scope of man; as
for carrying conviction, how can one do this, unless
to those who understand and have known for themselves, and learned the language of the hills? That
critic, I hope, earnest as he was, can never have
strayed into the places where I find wonder; or
else, perhaps, he strayed there and found nothing.
Let not that make him doubt that I found some-

thing there. We all find different things in life;
and the best of us the most. Having found one's
little, one can only offer; small matter whether one
be thought inadequate or a fraud; one is, as I say,
bound to be the one, and in one's efforts almost
bound to be thought the other, by the wrong
people. For my offer only holds good for those
who share the secret already; and I do not fear
from them an accusation of straying from the "real
thing," or, indeed, of committing any crime except
that of spreading mysteries too freely in the sight
of multitudes that may not have eyes to see or ears
to hear.

Down on the other side of the Antermoja Pass,
round yet another face of the Kesselkogel, goes the
pass; I diverged from where the track should run
over shingles now hidden by snowfields, to inspect
the enormous dank cliffs in vain for *Campanula
Morettiana* (I had believed this to be the Antermojakogel, on which it is reported); but *Androsace
Haussmanni* was there; and in the open rocks
along which we had just passed, above a little lake,
it was in flower, wizen and poor, nothing to distract
one's eyes from the view across the world from that
very high place. Failing of my Campanula, I
returned down a tumble of vast broken rosy blocks

to where the track again became evident far below, in a waste of level stone, with cairns put up to mark the way. This small Alpine plateau, still as if no life had ever made its appearance yet upon the earth, was strangely fascinating, its fine grey surface of shingle thickly darkly dotted with small sombre humps of vegetation—minute Willows, short-leaved Gentian far from its flower, and *Saxifraga cæsia* in that fine form which is so frequent in the Dolomites. This upland plain is the parent of waters destined for the Fassathal, and lies under the walls of the Seekogel and the Kesselkogel. Continuing across its weird expanse, you come suddenly upon the lovely, silent Antermoja Lake, lying cold and green and clear, full of transparent melting icebergs of emerald and crystal, some 8,000 feet above the sea. At its farther end a tiny club-hut was then building, and by now is certainly open to public use. If only the flowers hereabouts were of a more exciting nature it would be a glorious spot to come and stay—if, indeed, it be a place at which you *can* stay, and not merely an eating-refuge like the Taramelli, with food supplies, but no sleeping accommodation.

After the Antermoja Lake all is downhill, and a bathos and sad declension out of those wonderful

clean places—down into the swarming valleys again
and the countless tiresomenesses of man. One
crosses a windy shoulder and then down ; and over
again to the left, and down once more, until one
leaves the beautiful territory of rock for ever, and
descends upon dull Alps of unbroken green. But
before you drop so low there is one last presence,
the sovereign of them all, for you to take leave of
before you go. For, coming down from the Antermoja, as you round the shoulder of the near hill
and emerge upon the Antermoja Lake, there in
front of you, across the cold, clear water, and over
the intervening ranges and their valleys, rises the
profile of the Marmolata in supreme magnificence
at the end, lonely and dominating, throwing back
her vast glacier like a veil behind the dome of her
brow, and fronting the south in the sheer and brutal
glory of her unbroken cliff. This is the closing
view that this Dolomite tour will have to offer you,
and perhaps the most wonderful there is. And
hardly less wonderful and fearful to me is the
mystery as to why this aspect of the Marmolata
remains apparently untouched either by painters
or postcards. Is it possible that painters and
photographers are reluctant about coming so high ?
The fact remains that though you can get scores

of postcards and scores of sketches of the Marmolata's fat and comparatively undistinguished
northern full-face, I had to search far before we
could come on a photograph of that superb and
serene profile ; while as for sketches, I have never
yet seen any at all except Churchill's drawing
from the Sasso di Damm.

So now, filled to exhaustion with the mountain
air, we turn round a rocky shoulder and drop past
stone-slopes where, among the yellow Poppies,
Haussmann's Androsace is growing as freely as a
weed (and is nearly as dull, though not half as
ample), and so, again, round a crest of grass, at
once to find ourselves on black volcanic dust and
rock, where the violet and gold of *Linaria
alpina*, unseen before, blazes forth at you immediately, like a purple flame. After that it is
down and down into the upper Alpine reaches of
the Duronthal, and after that down and down
and down once more over meadow and through
forest, with the tortured fires of the Langkofel
shooting up above your head on the left, until,
sooner than you had dared to hope, a village comes
into sight in the Fassathal at your feet, and,
contrary to your warmest hopes, proves to be
Campitello, where, if you are wise, you do not

stay, but charter a fly to carry your tired feet a
mile or so forward to Canazei. It would be an
insult to feet acclimatized by now to the splendours of the Antermoja, to make them tramp
that miserable trodden highroad. Boots that had
weathered the screes of the Kesselkogel might
well burst with indignation at such a final outrage.
And at Canazei you resume the motor, and are
conveyed over the Pordoi again, and over the
Falzarego to Cortina on your homeward way to
Toblach, unless, indeed, you prefer the southerly
direction, and go round over by Cavalese and the
Cold Fountains once more so as to have one last
sight of Fräulein Anni and Fräulein Fanni before
you take the Brenner express from beloved Bozen.

Thus you have now reached the term of your
tour ; I hope the things I have told you may some
of them prove useful, even if they be not orna-
mental. I pretend only to take you among some
of the places I have visited and most love ; but
there are countless other peaks and huts and passes
as delightful as those I have named. As for com-
piling a guide-book or complete vade-mecum to the
Dolomites, what fool is there so great a fool as to
pretend intimate knowledge of one mountain, let
alone a dozen ranges ? When I really know my

own Ingleborough I may begin to think myself more competent not to fall off the Dolomites ; till then I give you only my suggestions for ways by which you may attain both pleasure and profit, catering as much for the stern and aspiring as for those to whom Salegg and Paneveggio are joys ample and succulent and sufficient.

Of one thing I am sure : if word of mine help to allure you to the Dolomites you will return again and again, and bless the hour that brought you this book. So overmastering is the fascination of those wild weird peaks for all those whose eyes are unsealed to the wonder of the hills, whether from close at hand in the silence of the Antermoja Pass, or from such discreet distances as Cortina or the Virglwarte. As for ways and means, I have indicated such, as occasion served ; but I dare not trespass on the domain of Mr. Baedeker, in whose invaluable pages you will, of course, find every detail of terms and distances and directions. My own aim is chiefly to inspire you with a longing to wander in these parts ; and when once that craving is properly excited, I can confidently leave you to rough-hew the means and details for your-selves with the aid of authoritative guide-books.

But I am told I must not forbid you to lend my

works. I therefore withdraw that churlish and illiberal prohibition, on the condition that if you do lend them, it shall never be for long enough for the borrower to finish the volume. Thus he will be (or should be) so tantalized, I hope, by the charms of the unfinished tour, that he will know neither rest nor sleep until he has purchased a copy for himself. So we shall all grow fat.

Of writing of books there is, indeed, we are told, no end ; and in trying to appease all one's critics there is no more profit than in weaving ropes of the wild sea-sand. For some people, my methods are said to be too austere ; others, erudite and arid, reprobate a prattlesomeness in my pages, and accuse me of being too terribly at ease in Sion among the plants I talk of with so unbridled and personal an intimacy. And yet, if one tones down one's colours at both ends of the scale, one runs the risk of having no colours left in the picture at all, and pleasing nobody. Therefore, in dealing with such plants as appear in these pages, I have tried to heed only discreetly what has been said, and merely tempered the various winds of my enthusiasm to the countless shorn lambs (or raging lions) by whom an author is surrounded ; but may Heaven shield me from ever arriving at a dead calm !

And if only you who read have anything like the pleasure in this book that I have had in the writing, then I shall go on, never minding criticism, with an even more brazen serenity than before. For to write of things one loves for the benefit of those who love them too, is a pleasure beyond most other pleasures. Short of being among the hills themselves, there is no joy keener than to be taken back to them by memory. The presumed desire of the public has procured me this pleasure ; to the public accordingly I return my thanks and best efforts.

INDEX

THE END

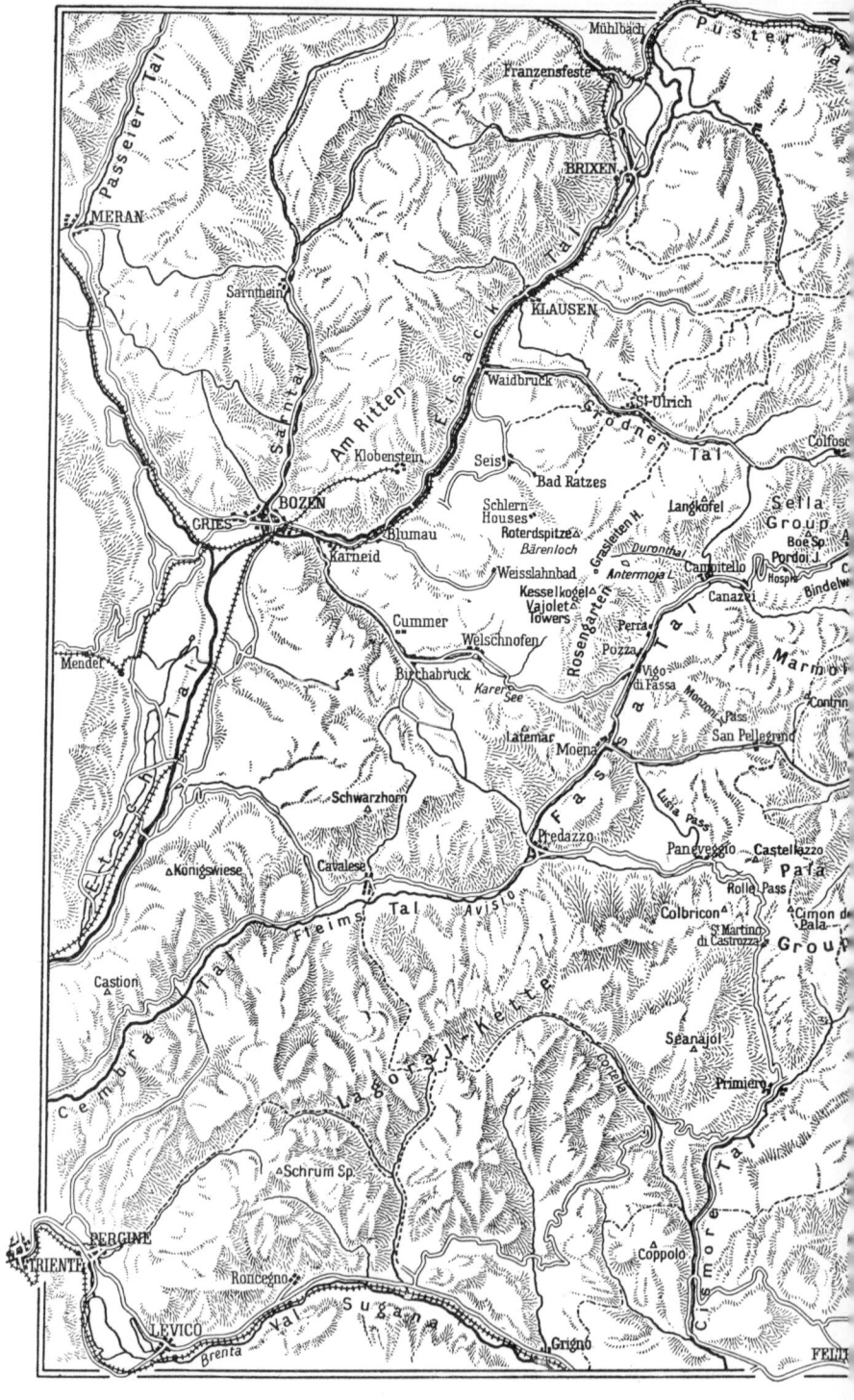

SKETCH MAP TO ACCOMPANY "THE DOLOMITES," BY E. HARRISON COMPTON AND R

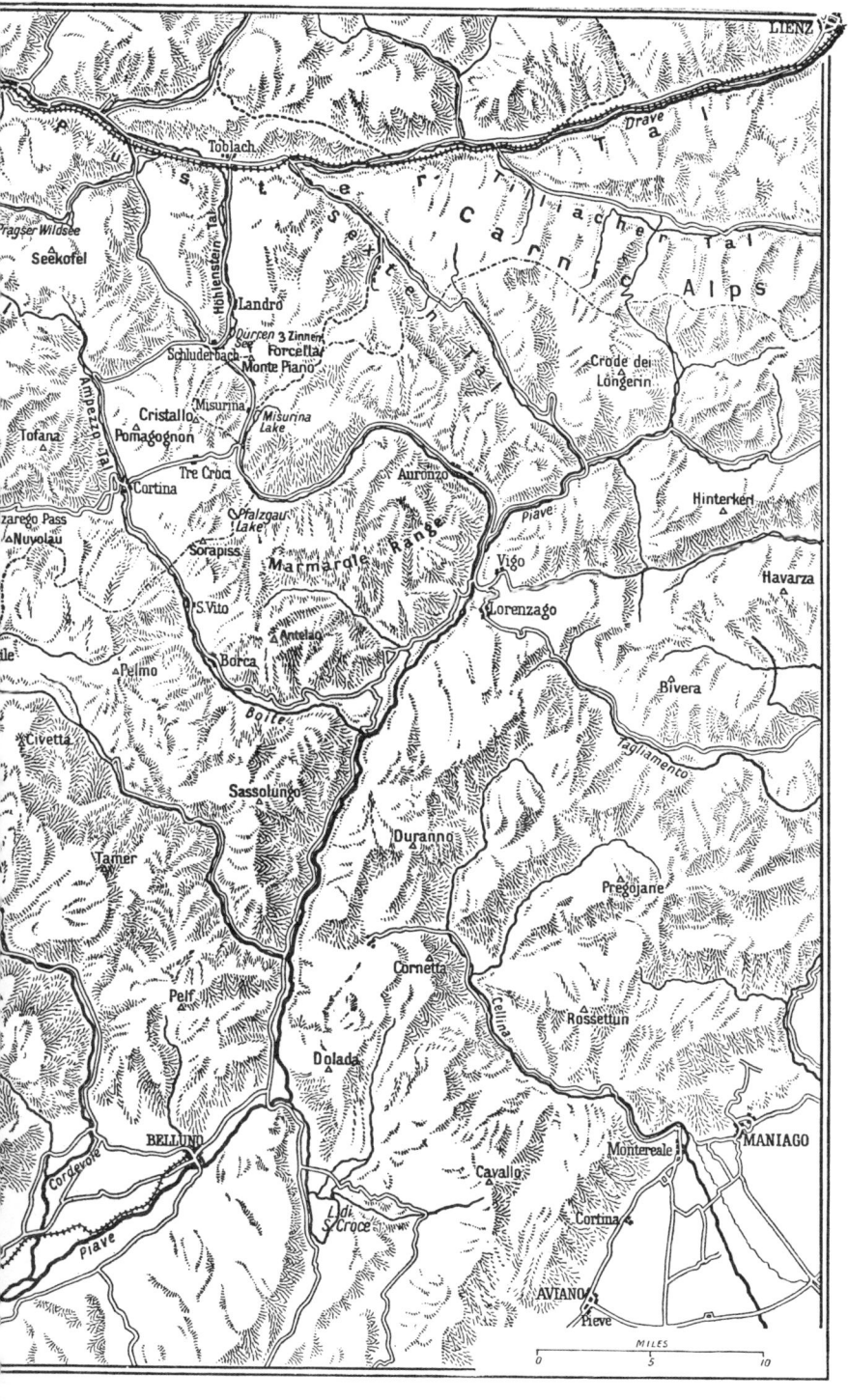